JACOB DINEZON

THE MOTHER AMONG OUR CLASSIC YIDDISH WRITERS

JACOB DINEZON
The Mother Among Our Classic Yiddish Writers

A Biography by
Shmuel Rozshanski

Translated from the Yiddish by
Miri Koral

Preface by
Scott Hilton Davis

Published by
Jewish Storyteller Press
2016

Jacob Dinezon photographs courtesy of
Archive of the YIVO Institute for Jewish Research, New York

Translated from
Yaakov Dinezon: Di mame tsvishn unzere klasikers
By Shmuel Rozshanski
Copyright © 1956 by Confederacion Pro Cultura Judia
Buenos Aires, Argentina
Argentinian Division of the International
Congress of Yiddish Culture

Permission to translate into English from
Confederacion Pro Cultura Judia—Fundación IWO

More information about Jacob Dinezon is available at
www.jacobdinezon.com

Published by
Jewish Storyteller Press
Raleigh, North Carolina U.S.A
www.jewishstorytellerpress.com
books@jewishstorytellerpress.com

ISBN 978-0-9798156-8-3

Library of Congress Control Number: 2016933831

For future literary historians.
May this translation be a springboard to further research.

TABLE OF CONTENTS

PREFACE

Jacob Dinezon was one of the most important Jewish writers of the mid-19th and early 20th centuries. He was a very successful novelist, and his sentimental potboiler, *The Dark Young Man*, is credited with being the first Yiddish bestseller.

Dinezon was also a major figure in the advancement of Yiddish as a literary language. He befriended or mentored almost every major Jewish writer of his day, including Abraham Goldfaden, the Father of Yiddish Theater; Sholem Abramovitsh, the Grandfather of modern Yiddish literature; Sholem Aleichem, the renowned humorist; S. Ansky, ethnographer and author of the supernatural play, *The Dybbuk*; and the poet, playwright, and master short story writer, I. L. Peretz, who became Dinezon's publishing partner and closest friend.

After a prolific career as an author—his collected works published after his death comprised eleven volumes—Dinezon spent the final years of his life caring for displaced children orphaned during the First World War. He also spearheaded the development of a secular Jewish schools movement in Eastern Europe.

When he died in 1919, tens of thousands of mourners poured out onto the streets of Warsaw to grieve the passing of their beloved folk writer and community philanthropist.

So, the question that always plagued me was how someone who was so closely associated with all the major Jewish writers of his day could be so completely neglected by contemporary literary historians, scholars, and academics? And you might say Jacob Dinezon and his mysterious disappearance from the discussion of modern Yiddish literature has become an obsession for me. When I first discovered his name while doing research on Sholem Aleichem and I. L. Peretz, I found my curiosity so aroused that I set forth to learn everything I could about this forgotten Yiddish writer.

What made the search for information about Jacob Dinezon so daunting was that none of his Yiddish novels or short stories had ever been translated into English. Important biographical entries, literary essays, and obituaries were also only in Yiddish. And because I don't speak or read Yiddish, it was necessary to find experts who could provide English translations.

Early in the research phase, it became clear that there was only one full-length biography about the life and work of Jacob Dinezon, and it, too, was in Yiddish: Shmuel Rozshanski's *Yaakov Dinezon: Di mame tsvishn unzere klasikers* (*Jacob Dinezon: The Mother Among Our Classic Yiddish Writers*).

What a strange title I thought, especially for someone who has been called the "Father of the Jewish Realistic Romance." Yet in his day, Rozshanski was a noted Yiddish literary historian, and his heavily footnoted work on Dinezon's life and career seemed an invaluable resource for future scholars.

Now, with permission from the Confederacion Pro Cultura Judia—Fundación IWO, and the encouragement of the Rollansky family in Israel, we are able to bring this Yiddish volume into the 21st century through the English translation of Miri Koral, founder and executive director of the California Institute for Yiddish Culture and Language and lecturer in Yiddish at the University of California, Los Angeles.

* * * * *

Shmuel Rozshanski (Samuel Rollansky) was born in Warsaw in 1902 and moved to Argentina with his family in 1922, three years after Dinezon's passing. Although he doesn't mention it in this biography, Rozshanski may have observed the outpouring of grief accompanying Dinezon's funeral in 1919.

Settling in Buenos Aires, Rozshanski (1902-1995) became a successful newspaper columnist, theater critic, short story writer, scholar, and editor of works in Yiddish. For many years he contributed a daily column to *Di yidishe tsaytung* (*The Jewish Newspaper*), and served as the director of the YIVO Institute for Yiddish Research in Argentina (IWO) and the Buenos Aires section of the Kultur Kongress (Culture Congress). He was also a central figure in the founding of organizations and activities advancing Yiddish literature and culture in Argentina and Latin America.

Shmuel Rozshanski's greatest legacy may be his contributions as editor and writer of introductions for the hundred-volume series, *Musterverk fun der yidisher literatur* (*Masterwork from the Yiddish Literature*), which featured works by important Yiddish authors and introduced readers to a vast collection of Yiddish literature.

Although not a part of the *Musterverk* series, Rozshanski published *Jacob Dinezon: The Mother Among Our Classic Yiddish Writers* in 1956 as a way of placing Jacob Dinezon in league with the three authors who had become known as the "classic writers" of modern Yiddish literature: Sholem Abramovitsh, Sholem Aleichem, and I. L. Peretz.

In a tribute to Sholem Abramovitsh, Sholem Aleichem had dubbed him "*der zayde*" (the grandfather) of Yiddish literature, and added himself to the lineage as "grandson." Scholars completed the "family tree" by calling I. L. Peretz the "father." In a bold move, Rozshanski suggests Dinezon should be considered the "mother" among these classic writers due to his kindhearted, gentle, and supportive nature.

Our purpose in publishing this English translation by Miri Koral is to add to the growing archive of information about Jacob Dinezon that is now available online at www.jacobdinezon.com

and also in book form. Our hope is that this volume will lead to additional research on Jacob Dinezon and other Jewish writers who played major roles in the creative explosion of Yiddish literature and culture at the turn of the 20th century.

Scott Hilton Davis
July 2016

JACOB DINEZON

THE MOTHER AMONG OUR CLASSIC YIDDISH WRITERS

ONE

A SWEET MAN IN A TRYING TIME

The spirit of the age and the spirit of people. — From Ribal
to Mendele. — Satirists. — A *Maskil* with leniency. — Peretz's
characteristics. — Naïveté among keen sages. — Dinezon's novel:
"Whispered Prayer." — Last confession.

Among the Yiddish writers of the 19th century Jacob Dinezon was unique. He was unique in character, unique in his life,
and especially unique in his writing.

He was a *maskil*—a proponent of the *Haskalah* (Jewish Enlightenment)—and yet entirely naïve, bashful, modest, sentimental,
and virtuous. He demonstrated how Hasidic fanaticism led to
tragedy, yet did so without rancor or displaying any bitterness toward the corrupt people he described.

When his first novels initially appeared in the 1870s and
1880s, Yiddish writers were either loudly condemning and "tearing
out pieces" of the old-fashioned behaviors, or laughing uproariously
at the bleakness and societal transgressions in the Jewish shtetls. It
was still fashionable to be bitterly condemning, as was Ribal (Isaac
Baer Levinsohn), the theorist of the *Haskalah* in Russia. They were
not yet free of the impression that Linetski made by his insulting
and sullying of Hasidism. And if Mendele Mocher Sforim's sharp
satires weren't as shocking, it was only thanks to his writerly craft,
mastery of style, and playfulness by which the learned man
scorched. In general, however, there roiled the same acrimony in
literature as in life.

15

"One need only look back at Jewish life from earlier times. One need only remember and truly imagine: Beggarsville, Poverty-town, Seven-Muddies, Hypocriteville, and the total chaos of old Jewish 'cities and shtetls.'"[1]

It was at this time that Jacob Dinezon arrived and, instead of acrimony, he brought sentimentalism. Instead of the letter of the law, he brought leniency.

"He speaks brother-to-brother, quite often like a mother to a beloved child. The way one needed to speak to the sick ghetto-children."[2]

His novels described shady characters, but in juxtaposition to each dark figure, he presented a positive character. He even refrained from expressing his hatred of the people he presented as devils who brought sorrow, troubles, and tragic death to his beloved heroes.

Jacob Dinezon was a gentle, refined Jew who couldn't tolerate any offense. Therefore, he protected himself: he avoided giving offense or being offended himself.

Dinezon was far removed from socialist theories. The idea of class warfare was foreign to him. However, one can find in his works many pages which were used by socialists, anarchists, and communists in the form of ideas and suggestions to counter social injustice in Jewish life.

Although he limited his hatred against dark characters, he drenched with affection those that he loved: characters with honorable, naïve, childish natures—victims of bloated egotists and wild fanatics.

"J. Dinezon is the optimist in our Yiddish literature. For him, wickedness is merely an accident, and he is certain that goodness will always triumph over life's unfortunate circumstances."[3] This is

---

[1] I. L. Peretz, "Jacob Dinezon," 1903, *The Works of I. L. Peretz,* 1920, NY, p. 132.
[2] Ibid, p. 135.
[3] Bal-Makhshoves ("The Thinker"; pseudonym of Isidor Eliashev), *Selected Writings,* Vilna, 1910, Vol. 1, "Jacob Dinezon (On His 25th Anniversary)," p. 116.

how he was considered at the beginning of the 20th century. This is also how he appears today from a distance, many years after his passing. At present one has to fathom the distance—what a span it is from his writerly beginnings!

In his day, Jacob Dinezon was utterly unique in his optimism. "Enlightened ones," therefore, regarded him with a smile that implied, "What a naïve person!"

However, Jacob Dinezon was on the outside exactly as he was on the inside: a sweet person in a trying time. He didn't feel embarrassed being a childishly modest man among circles of keen sages.

*　*　*　*　*

The tale of a single novel characterizes Dinezon as both writer and person.

Dinezon, born in Nay-Zhager, near Kovno, in the true Lithuania, became an orphan at age twelve, and after his father's death, he went to live with an uncle in the Greater Russian city of Mohilev. Stemming from a pedigreed family, he was soon introduced to the world of Holy Scripture and books. In Mohilev, he studied in the synagogue's yeshiva and, under the influence of *maskilim* there, devoted himself to secular studies, which included Hebrew literature, Russian, and German. These particular bodies of knowledge led him to take up teaching, in which he was fortunate. As a young man, he was accepted as a tutor in one of the richest and most important families in Mohilev, the Horowitzes, for whom he later became the administrator, bookkeeper, and business manager.

Bodaneh Horowitz, the lady of the house, had a splendid pedigree. She was a native of Vilna and came from an important and rich family of *maskilim*. Her sister was the wife of Romm, the famous Vilna printer of holy books.

Bodaneh Horowitz made her home an important cultural and social center for awakened youths and intelligentsia. All the heavy hearted would seek support there, and there was no shortage of heavy hearts at that time. While in this city near the Dnieper River there was no great concentration of Hasidim, and the Orthodox Jews were less fanatical than in the small towns, there were, however, constant bitter conflicts and dramatic clashes between parents and children.

Revolutionary spirits captivated the young; the respectable *Haskalah* beckoned and drew to it young men and women. Many parents who "caught" their children reading "little gentile books" were immediately convinced that they were heading, God forbid, directly to conversion. So the clashes were such that the escape of children in the middle of the night became a frequent occurrence, and there were worse misfortunes, even to the point of suicide.

Bodaneh Horowitz's home became a center for this awakened youth. Gathered there were influential *maskilim* and idealistic men of business who comprehended the conflicts and sought ways to help with money, advice about family matters, papers to travel abroad or, if they were dealing with talented young people, opportunities for stimulation, learning, and morale boosting.

It was in this home that Jacob Dinezon became tutor to the Horowitz's only daughter, an accomplished young girl who demonstrated great skill as a pianist. And it is with this girl that the tutor fell in love.

The tutor, however, did not reveal to anyone what he felt for his student. He kept it a holy secret and didn't say a word to the girl. He suffered, but never disclosed anything. He was in an agony of distress, but never said a word to anyone.

Most likely, Dinezon kept to the pedagogic principle that a teacher cannot take advantage of his student's trust and sense of authority. And exactly for that reason, because of his privileged position, he was obligated to keep a distance—especially since he was a trusted employee of the entire family. As the tutor, he was privy to consultations regarding the most intimate family matters. He was also called upon when decisions had to be made about sending their only daughter to Vienna to study with a great professor of piano. He had to give his opinion, yet he didn't say one word about what was weighing on his heart. This is how he bid her farewell, although afterwards he did seek to unburden his heart by traveling to Vienna.

Dinezon also wanted to travel to Breslov to enter the seminary for rabbis. For *maskilim* in those days, such travels for the purpose of studying were very common. The Horowitzes, however, did not permit it. He was such a trusted manager, they needed him for their own affairs. And he didn't have the strength to hurt them. So he stayed until their only daughter, after three years of study in Vienna and Paris, returned to Mohilev. And when she returned, they began to arrange a match for her with a young cousin who was one of Romm's sons. And who should they send to iron out all the details of the match if not their tutor who was such a trusted man?

The aggrieved tutor remained silent at this juncture as well. Trust is trust. A mission is a mission. They, after all, trusted him implicitly! Since there was no indication of his love or his sorrow, should he affront them with his affection and demand his right to love?

The tutor remained silent until the end. He journeyed and carried out the mission that had been set before him. He came to an agreement as to when his beloved would marry another. Upon his return to Mohilev he spent several weeks in bed.[4]

This is the kind of teacher Jacob Dinezon was.

* * * * *

Did Jacob Dinezon think well of "whispered prayer"?

Certainly he must have had his unfortunate love affair in mind when, many years later, in 1911, he wrote in a letter from Warsaw to the critic S. Niger in Switzerland: "'Whispered prayer' is how

---

[4]S. L. Tsitron, *Three Literary Generations,* Vol. 1, "Jacob Dinezon," pp 56-104, Warsaw 1920.

the *shmone esrey* prayers are referred to, because one is not permitted to say them out loud. And do you know why? Because in *shmone esrey* there is also confession: 'Forgive us our Father because we have sinned, pardon us because we have transgressed!' Sins cannot be confessed out loud; before others we must not expose our sins. Don't you know that speaking or writing about everything that one did or even just dreamt about in one's youth is, for a person who doesn't want to fool himself, a type of confession of the sins of youth?"[5]

Only gentle souls can think like this. It's rare that people are tender to such a degree. This is the kind of gentle person that Jacob Dinezon was, and this is the kind of stirring humanity that he contributed to Yiddish literature and the literary canon of Jewish writers.

---

[5]"Jacob Dinezon's Letters" with commentary by S. Niger, *Di Tsukunft* (*The Future*), 1929, p. 621.

Two

WHY DID DINEZON THE HEBRAIST BECOME A YIDDISH WRITER?

From teacher to belletrist. — "First question." — The conflict between his mother and Michael Gordon about writing holy books and Yiddish songs. — "True *maskilim* are ashamed to write jargon." — The Nanny. — From compassion for the coarse world to the call of "my artistic soul." — How to be free of one's schooled religious texts in one's writing? — The popularizer wants to be independent. — Through Yiddish he became independent. — Embracing one's life.

Jacob Dinezon became involved with Yiddish literature as a cultivated teacher.

His closest friend, I. L. Peretz, thought of him more as a teacher of morals than as an artist: "First, that is, be liberal, good, and honorable; only afterwards, beautiful! The picture, the scene, the part of the described life is not a goal in and of itself. Life perhaps has no purpose in and of itself! The artist must therefore, at least, demonstrate that one must love another; that one's wrongdoing does not have to oppress another; that falseness, intrigues, fanaticism, bad habits, and the like do not lead to goodness; that 'Jewishness is not the magical belief in saints and their miracles.'"[6]

With this particular view of literature, Dinezon arrived at writing. And since he was a very naïve person, a tender, utterly honorable person, he understood nothing more than in order for

[6]*I. L. Peretz*, Vol. 10, p. 132.

someone to write, one must trust in life. From this arose a realism steeped in sentimentality.

* * * * *

In his memoir, which he began in 1911 in remembrance of S. Niger, Dinezon's introduction described an episode of his "first attempt at writing" that characterizes both himself and the time in which he lived.

He describes how, since childhood, he loved white paper. "What use it had for me," he says, "I had no idea. Yet, the moment I saw, either on the street or in *cheder,* a boy with a piece of empty, beautiful, and clean writing paper, no price—based on what I possessed then—was too dear."

One day, he "stole" several pieces of paper from his father's desk, and when asked why he did this, he found it impossible to reply. His father became angry and wanted to punish him, especially for the sake of his mother, who actually perceived this as little Jacob heading down a terrible path, dear God. The child, however, was lucky because their neighbor and good friend was the poet Michael Gordon, who saw an alternative explanation for this attraction to writing paper. As a result, there took place between Gordon and Dinezon's mother this conversation:

"What does he need the paper for? Why does he like it so much?" his mother asked.

"Perhaps, although the paper really isn't useful for anything yet, the fact that he is drawn to it is an indication the paper is somehow related to his young soul. Who can know what he will grow up to become? Maybe someday he will be a great rabbi and write holy books on paper about the Torah."

"From your mouth to God's ears!" Dinezon's mother declared.

Then Gordon added, "Or maybe he'll actually become an educated person and write the kinds of songs I write!"[7]

---

[7]Michael Gordon, *A Folk Poet From Vilna,* 1832-1890, is the author of the popular song, "The Whiskey."

To this Dinezon's mother replied: "You should better bite off your tongue!"[8]

* * * * *

"Better to bite off your tongue!" rather than become a Yiddish writer—this was the thinking in every respectable Jewish home in the 19th century. Even those who took pleasure in reading "jargonly writing" trembled at the thought of their child taking up writing in Yiddish. Like everyone else, Jacob Dinezon thought this as well.

Therefore, he first began writing articles and correspondences in Hebrew journals. In Yiddish, he wrote essays about natural science. In Hebrew he wanted to become a writer and in Yiddish a teacher.

"Several years after my leaving Warsaw," relates our greatest historian about the personal relationship and friendship that began in 1887, "Dinezon corresponded with me. All his letters were written in Hebrew. Writing in Russian was difficult for him, and according to the customs of those times, 'it didn't suit' to correspond in Yiddish between learned men who knew how to write in Hebrew. True *maskilim* were ashamed to write in jargon."[9]

Today, what is curious in the history of Yiddish literature and culture is what was said by the one who later became the flag-bearer of Yiddishism. Even in 1891, Peretz wrote in his foreword to the first volume of *Yiddish Library* that "Jargon doesn't have any pretensions of replacing the native position in a Jewish home. This position is occupied and needs to be occupied by Hebrew; jargon has no pretensions to the position of teaching, this position has eventually to be occupied by the language of the land. Jargon is only a nanny; she just wants to teach how to walk, sit, and begin to talk.

[8]"Reminders," "The Yiddish Record Book," *Yearbook of the History of Yiddish Literature and Language for Folklore, Critique and Bibliography,* First Edition, 1912, S. Niger editor, Vilna, p. 150.
[9]Simon Dubnow, *From "Jargon" to Yiddish,* Vilna 1929. "The Amiable Jacob Dinezon," pp. 24-32.

Then you can throw the nanny out, or, in gratitude, leave her a place at the table!"[10] If the revolutionary Peretz could assert this, then what could it mean for the proper Dinezon?

* * * * *

Then why, indeed, did Dinezon begin writing in Yiddish? He speaks about himself on the occasion of telling S. Niger about Isaac Meier Dik: "I saw my name printed with big letters for the first time under one of my articles in *Ha-Magid* (*The Preacher*), then in *Ha-Melitz* (*The Advocate*), in *Ha-Karmel* (*Mount Carmel*), *Ha-Tsefirah* (*The Morning*), and similarly in Smolensky's *Ha-Shakhar* (*The Dawn*). I first wrote in Yiddish whenever I felt like teasing, or to make myself and my friends merry, and in this way I gradually changed my mind to where there could be nothing more natural than writing in Yiddish for Jewish readers. Yiddish began to please both my artistic sensibility and my Jewish mind, which always troubled me when writing in Hebrew for only a small group of friends to whom I actually had nothing to say, nothing to recount.

"Yet the thousands and tens of thousands of brothers and sisters for whom my words might be useful and my tales might give pleasure could not hear my words or listen to my tales because I wrote in a language that only we savants, we learned ones, we enlightened ones understood; but not them, the ignorant upon whom we looked down from a great height."[11]

So Dinezon began to write in Yiddish out of compassion. With complete childish innocence he revealed those hidden thoughts that had tormented him. In other words, a transgressor! You could write in Yiddish and see how great the need was for your writing in Yiddish, yet you ignored the language and were ashamed of it. How could a Jew be so heartless?

[10] *I. L. Peretz,* "Education," Vol. 12, p. 17.
[11] "Jacob Dinezon's Letters," *Di Tsukunft* (*The Future*), 1929, No. 9.

Dinezon, however, confessed wholeheartedly that in the process of writing, while he was trying out his pen in both Hebrew and Yiddish, he began to realize that in actuality he was drawn to writing in Yiddish not so much out of compassion, but for another reason: he started to feel that as good a Hebraist as he was, his Hebrew didn't flow. While on the other hand, as little as it befit him to lower himself to writing in Yiddish, his Yiddish flowed.

"My artistic soul," he recounts, "couldn't remain satisfied from writing in Hebrew because it seemed to feel constrained and not free. Not because words and expressions were missing. Those I had more than enough of in my Hebrew Bible, and exactly those overly abundant and ready words in their usage had blocked their own freethinking, and instead of speaking for myself, Isaiah, Job, or Ecclesiastes always spoke for me. At other times with my Hebrew, I clothed my protagonists in strange, ill-suited clothes. The clothes hung worn and awkward, and I myself was no more than a second-hand clothes dealer. I felt entirely different in Yiddish. Here no one was speaking for me, not Isaiah, not even Ezekiel. I spoke for myself, and not only did I speak for myself, but my protagonists also spoke in their own tongue, each one as he felt and was used to speaking. I didn't have to search for words and expressions for them, especially ones which they had never lost."[12]

Dinezon transitioned from Hebrew to Yiddish the way a son leaves his father when he wants to become independent. His father is actually kind and good, but the child still wants to become independent. Yiddish helped those Jewish writers become independent who were drawn to their people but couldn't make an intimate connection using Hebrew.

This is how the "artistic soul," as Dinezon expressed it, oriented the young *maskil* to his path. Although he began writing in Yiddish when he "felt like teasing to enliven himself and his friends," he "gradually came to the conclusion that there does not

[12]Ibid.

exist anything more natural than writing in Yiddish for Jewish readers," and Yiddish began to satisfy his "artistic sentiments."

If Dinezon had simply relied on his logic and highly regarded teaching, he certainly wouldn't have become the noted author he became. He might have made a number of additional translations relating universal and Jewish history,[13] he might have published a few more brochures and booklets which informed about countries and peoples, as well as the natural sciences, for which he had a special weakness.[14] Perhaps he would have also printed booklets about accounting and trade.[15] All these would have been published in an affected style, as was the custom among his circle of *maskilim*.[16]

As a Hebraist, although sharper and more categorical than others who wrote in Hebrew before they transitioned to Yiddish, Dinezon couldn't compare himself to I. L. Peretz, who "already then wrote a wonderful Hebrew" and "was both the adored and wild child of those *maskilic* societies."[17] However, even Peretz wound up in Yiddish. So, for all the more reasons, did Dinezon.

A writer must succeed at choosing his own path, just as every human being must succeed at choosing a profession.

* * * * *

[13]Gretz's *Folk History of the Jews* and Vol. 1, "World History" (printed as a supplement to *Jew* in 1900) was the beginning of a wide-ranging opus that created among Jews a greater understanding of their history.

[14]His brochure, "Thunder and Lightning," was published in 1876. Later, "Rain and Snow," "Egypt," "Babel," "Vienna," "The Mormons: Their Religion and Their History." Dinezon also refined a series of lectures about natural sciences based on Bernstein.

[15]Dinezon was for many years a bookkeeper which he likely learned in Mohilev from his uncle who had a reputation as a mathematician.

[16]Beginning with his uncle, Isaac Eliashev, who was truly observant, but at the same time was involved in secular knowledge and languages.

[17]Nokhum Sokolov, *Personalities,* translated by Moses Shender, Polish Jewry Press, Buenos Aires, 1948, "I. L. Peretz," pp. 20 and 37.

But between a teacher and a writer there is an obvious difference. A teacher can satisfy himself by repeating what others say. A writer can't gain any enjoyment from copying and repeating. And a writer who has no enjoyment from his own writing can't bring about enjoyment in others.

One can learn how to write, but one cannot learn how to become a writer. One can learn how to speak well, but one cannot learn to be an orator. To become one yourself, one has to bring something to it beyond what is inherited; something attained from learning, or from the street, life, or experience. A writer must always be in the process of becoming. It has to always come to him. If it doesn't come, it languishes.

Just like culture, a writer can't "remain in place." If there is no movement forward, there is no "remaining in place"—the movement is backwards. Living means creating. An alive writer is comparable to someone on a mountain for the first time—either he climbs higher, further, or he falls down, slides down, crashes down. "Remaining in place" one can only do when one goes forward, however little, but forward—and alone!

When Dinezon tried to write in Yiddish he felt that he wrote on his own and liberated himself from the Scriptures and the affected style which, in his day, held sway over everyone learned in Hebrew. Instead of speaking in the abstract, he began to write from the life that arose before him, that he himself observed, that he himself felt. Instead of making something up, it is better to describe what springs from life; to join in, empathize, and become intimately involved.

In Yiddish, Jacob Dinezon immediately managed to evoke a sense of intimacy. Both he and his reader instantly sensed the warmth of blood, heart, restlessness, sorrow, and too little joy. In Yiddish, life spoke to him everywhere in the most sentimental tones.

Three

A NEW TYPE OF *MASKIL*:
INSTEAD OF INSULTING HE LAMENTS
THE BELOVED AND PLEASING

For the Sins of the Fathers. — The tragic conflict between parents and
children. — Dinezon's meeting Isaac Meier Dik. — The prohibition
of the censor. — A disappointing mistake about his second novel. —
He finds out in Moscow about the publication of *The Beloved and
Pleasing* and its great success. — The new elements that captivated. —
Style, approach, and implementation of another Enlightenment. —
A new way of pleasing the public: the evildoer is victorious and the
refined folks depart this earth. — The popularity of crying.

In confronting life, Jacob Dinezon, as a *maskil*, observed that in
the conflict between children and their parents, the parents were
more to blame. In fact, the children, who were presented as un-
abashedly insolent, were merely victims of their fanatical, obtuse
parents who refused to understand that time doesn't stand still.

Life supplied him with this sad testimony: a true story. A rich
man in the city of Mohilev forced his gifted, sensitive daughter
into marriage with an uncouth boy. The daughter belonged to the
circle of intelligent youth that found a home at the Horowitzes
where Dinezon was the tutor and, later, bookkeeper. She was
steeped in literature, wrote poems, and evoked her personal drama
in poetry. From the outset, she waged war with her father, but in
the end decided to marry the uncouth lad, hoping that she would
be able in time to change him so that he wouldn't embarrass her in

public. Shortly after the wedding, however, there arose a great scandal: while they were out in public together, he made a terrible scene that so affected the sensitive young woman that she escaped to a horse stall and hanged herself.

This true story was used by Dinezon for his first novel, which he entitled, *Bevn Oves* (*For the Sins of the Fathers*). This was in 1874. Dinezon at that time happened to travel to Vilna on a mission for the Horowitzes to their relatives the Romms. He traveled to their home as if he were a member of the family. At the Romms, there were always visitors, including such notable Hebrew and Yiddish writers as Isaac Meier Dik, Kalman Shulman, Adam Hakohen Lebenson, and Samuel Joseph Pin. Dik was a gold mine for Romm's press, although he barely earned anything from this to live on.[18] However, Dik's popularity was greatly accepted even by the well educated.

Dinezon's meeting with Dik, their conversations, and Dik's praise about writing in Yiddish, therefore, made a deep impression on the young writer.[19] Especially when Dik, having read Dinezon's first work, offered such warm opinions, the young author blushed hotly. It was actually on Dik's recommendation that *For the Sins of the Fathers* was accepted by the Romm Press to be published in book form. What's more, the Romms gave Dinezon his honorarium way in advance, paying him exactly what they paid the famous and beloved Isaac Meier Dik.

Yet, Dinezon's disappointment was great when a while later he was told that the novel couldn't be published because the censor's reading of the manuscript rendered it forbidden. Why? S. L. Tsitron, one of Dinezon's oldest friends, describes how the censor, whose name was Vohl, saw in his reading the tragedy of his own relative.

[18]"Contract with Romm Publishing," No. 2, *From the Recent Past*, Warsaw 1937.
[19]In an afore-cited letter, Dinezon says about Dik, "More natural would be if the butcher women at the butchers or fishmongers at the fish market all spoke, swore and cursed in Hebrew, in true Isaiah-language, rather than in good, dear, all around loyal, and warm Yiddish in which Isaac Meir Dik spoke to his Vilna Jews and Jewesses."

So he used his privileged position to forbid the circumstances from becoming widely known.[20]

But Dinezon's disappointment over his first written novel did not come to the same end as the first romance in his life.

*   *   *   *   *

When Dinezon presented his *For the Sins of the Fathers* to the Romm Press, he also brought a second novel, *The Beloved and Pleasing, or The Dark Young Man.*

A bothersome error has been spread regarding this novel: that Dinezon—as is stated in several important books—wrote his second novel most likely to pay off his debt to the publishing house. According to one source, first surfacing in 1920, the novel "was finished in less than one month."[21] Eight years later, the curious story was further spread in this form: "In order to cover the honorarium that he received for the censored *For the Sins of the Fathers*, Dinezon, in the space of six weeks, from Passover to Shavuot, finished off his second novel, *The Beloved and Pleasing, or the Dark Young Man*, Vilna 1877, 240 pages."[22]

This particular error leaves room to imagine Dinezon's approach to literature as being different from what it was and is not true. He himself laughed off those who "write literature for a ruble, for a gulden, and for a kopeck," as long as they are told, "Write and take an honorarium!"[23]

In truth, Dinezon wrote his second novel even before he knew that his first would be censored. What's more, Dinezon made this matter perfectly clear in his autobiographical letter to S. Niger in

---

[20]"Though he scratched out and found quite a different excuse" for the government. S. L. Tsitron, *Three Literary Generations,* Vol. 1, pp. 68.

[21]Ibid, pp. 69. Dinezon's friend, the socialist revolutionary Alezer (Eliezer?) Zukerman, told of this happening, however, in the form of a diary, known as "Upside Down World," in *Ha-Shakhar* (*The Dawn*), Year 6.

[22]Zalman Reisen, *Lexicon of Yiddish Literature, Press, and Philology,* Vilna 1928, Vol. 1, Column 701.

[23]*Memories and Scenes,* Warsaw 1937, "Deception," p. 209.

1911. He writes: "Purchased from me by the publishers, the Widow and Brothers Romm, exactly just this *For the Sins of the Fathers*. *The Dark Young Man* they took from me entirely due to *For the Sins of the Fathers*, but not to print. I was told by the business manager, Mr. Feigenson, who explained that it was just to remain at the press's archive should the appropriate time arrive for it to be worth publishing also."

The picture becomes even clearer in Dinezon's memoir, where he describes how he found himself in Moscow "serving as a clerk in a popular tea company" and "couldn't know that there in Vilna, truly at the famous publishers Widow and Brothers Romm, there lay about a few of my 'manuscripts,' and perhaps one of them was already being printed and being circulated in the world. And the more I thought about it," he confesses in full, "the more I wanted no one close to me to find out about it."[24] Under these circumstances, a day later, to his great astonishment, he happens to hear this story from a Moscow bookseller:

"Just a few weeks ago, a Hebrew-translation (Yiddish) book was published with the name *The Beloved and Pleasing* in Hebrew, and immediately with a commentary, *or the Dark Young Man*. And there occurred something of a run on it: the first hundred copies were immediately snatched up from me in merely three days. So I sent a dispatch to Vilna: 'Send me, through livery, as I indicated in my first dispatch, another three hundred. In less than a week not even one remains.' And they sent me another one hundred and fifty pieces with the notice that there are no more left in Vilna either."

And the bookseller, in his great desire for success, calls out: "It all depends on luck, even a little Yiddish book! Heaven and earth and *The Dark Young Man*."[25]

[24]"Sholem Jacob Abramovitsh and Mendele Mocher Sforim," in *Memories and Scenes*, p. 179.
[25]Ibid., pp. 184-5.

The bookseller was especially surprised that the writer was an unknown and that this little book was his first. In other words, why did he not know such an author? In those days, every author would tread the thresholds of every bookseller when his piece of literature was published. And here comes an unknown who has such success!

Jacob Dinezon, the most unassuming of all, unwittingly became the most successful novelist of his day, even before there were daily Yiddish newspapers, and before Jewish life in hundreds of shtetls was awakened from its habitual slumber.

* * * * *

Dinezon's enormous success with his first published novel derived from the new approach that readers, especially female readers, encountered in his work. In a drawn-out style, slowly and in detail, Dinezon hit an intimate tone. Using folksy language, mixing in Russian words that were in common use among the masses, and with Hebrew passages that were known to every observant Jew, Dinezon immediately interjected into his narrative a sense of familiarity that came through the homey relationship readers had with the characters he described.

With sugar-sweet prose, the novelist presented his beloved heroes—beautiful, warm, truly righteous—in opposition to whom he presented a type of bad guy, a Dark Young Man, for whom all means were kosher so long as he reached his goal. As the evil one's plot unfolded, the dramatic tension built and captured the reader.

For those who were not yet raised with artistic literature, what was captivating and disturbing was the primitive form of presenting extremes: black and white opposites wrapped in great sentimentality and executed with the ease of a true folk writer.

But what was so new was the writer's approach to his protagonists. In contrast to vulgar writers who mostly wanted to satisfy the desires of the mass reader, and, therefore, punished the evildoers and gave happy outcomes to the good folks, Dinezon demonstrated that, as a result of violation and torment, good folks often have quite a bad end while the evildoers live well, because despite their sins and offenses, they are the most important bosses of the town.

Dinezon, however, did not incite against the evildoer. Instead, he showed him in the blackest colors so that the evildoer was engraved in the memory of the reader for the rest of his life. But he did not elicit rage. Instead, he calmed his readers by arousing tears for his beloved, honorable, and gentle heroes.

The title is enough to know where he places his emphasis. At first Dinezon gives the title, *The Beloved and Pleasing.* Only then comes *The Dark Young Man.*

Joseph, the yeshiva boy, has every virtue. Rosa is a refined maiden. Her brother-in-law, the Dark Young Man of the title, can't abide the tender couple's falling in love. So he tells on them. The girl's parents then force her to marry a worthless fellow, and Joseph, exactly like the biblical Joseph, serves time in prison. But he returns, and Rosa's sister, Rekhama, becomes his lover. Once again ideal! But the Dark Young Man is still in opposition. Just when their luck seems imminent, the evildoer sets the house on fire. Joseph catches a fever and perishes, his lover languishes and dies of sorrow, and the Dark Young Man becomes an important man about town.

Other *maskilim,* in telling such a story, would strike a different chord by insulting the unsavory characters that drive the honorable ones to their early graves. Dinezon, on the contrary, put his emphasis on the unfortunate ones: he lamented them. So is it any wonder that the pages of the novel became soaked in readers' tears?

The ten thousand copies of the novel that were shortly spread over Russia allow us to see: one, that the Jewish masses found their writer in Dinezon; two, that they yearned to find something that mirrored their own lives and bitter conflicts; and three, that one could win over the public with goodness more than with curses and damnations.

FOUR

THE AUTHOR WHO IS FRIGHTENED
BY HIS GREAT SUCCESS

A novel and slogan. — The profound disturbance. — New readers. —
An opposite outcome: the more popular, the more sorrow. — An
invasion of lowbrow imitators. — The fear of writing again. — Why
did the Hebrew press ignore *The Beloved and Pleasing, or the Dark Young
Man*? — Dinezon's desire to show off for the Hebraists and Smolensky's
attack against Yiddish. — The difficult atmosphere for a Yiddish writer.

The Beloved and Pleasing, or the Dark Young Man widely disturbed the Jewish masses in hundreds of cities and towns across
Tsarist Russia. It became famous. Shedding tears over the young
folks in love—over Joseph, Rosa, Rekhama, the victims of backwardness and intrigues—became for girls, and even boys, a profound
experience.[26] After reading the novel, young people couldn't sleep
at night and during the day they walked around in a daze.

The deep disturbance that the novel aroused in its readers was
described at length in a strange scene in one of S. Ansky's novels
wherein someone wanted to console his friends who were heart-
broken after finishing Dinezon's *The Beloved and Pleasing*. The
character comforted them by saying that only in the novel is it so
sad. In reality, as he knows, the story ended quite differently. Firstly,
Joseph didn't die; he recovered from the fever and remained alive.
Secondly, he married his beloved. Thirdly, the "Dark Young Man"
didn't improve his situation but came to a very bad end: he was

[26]Peretz Hirschbein, *My Childhood*, 1932, p. 261.

35

sent off to do forced labor for swindling. "You hear this?" said one of the listeners who jumped up and ran off to "tell Khasye" because "it will make her happy!"[27]

To weep and become happy. The tears caused enjoyment.

Rarely has a book had such a profound effect on a reading public as did Dinezon's first published novel. Thanks to him, the "jargonist" literature drew many new readers. *The Dark Young Man* became a slogan: this is what anyone willing to perpetrate a bad deed in order to reach his goal was thusly called.

* * * * *

But the more popular and adored *The Dark Young Man* became, and the more the book was sought after for purchase and reading, the less pleasure the author Jacob Dinezon experienced.

He was even more dismayed by the silence of the Hebrew press, which ignored his book even though it interested the widest public. He grew upset by the satiric words of the Jewish Enlightenment intelligentsia about this kind of sentimental novel that elicited so many tears. His hurt blossomed over the fact that they came from those from whom he most wanted to hear praise—because he wanted to belong to them just as his soul belonged—yet they ignored or made fun of his work. His mood grew bizarre: the greater his success, the greater his sorrow. He became plagued with this idea: should he have written it at all? Then he concluded: no more writing. Why? Because he had only shame and disgrace from his novel.

As if this weren't enough, he began noticing the appearance of imitative works by those who were envious of his success. In the marketplace, wild storybooks showed up by authors who tried to gain an audience using his manner of writing. Ugly writings and lowbrow novels appeared that disgusted him and seemed to degrade the Yiddish language.

[27]S. Ansky, "Pioneers," *A Chronicle of the 70s*, Vol. 2, Vilna 1927, pp. 139-141.

Dinezon writes about this in his autobiographical sketch to S. Niger: "Regarding the popularity of *The Dark Young Man*, I believe you have much less information. Practically in the same year I finished my novel *Even Negef,* I had already lost the desire to publish it. There was dead silence on the part of the selfsame official Jewish press about my work, though tens of thousands had been sold with barely a Jewish house where this work wasn't read. In addition, there were all sorts of writing businesses that the success of my work created, and it was the inspiration for all kinds of novels and storybooks in a similar style, especially Shomer with his exaggerated praise of rich beggars and the like, to the extent of dozens every morning. Regarding *The Dark Young Man*, I was affected so badly that I felt guilty for this entire flood of empty and meaningless novels in which the Yiddish reader was drowning. I couldn't stop writing, but not publishing what I wrote didn't cost me any special effort or spiritual strain."[28]

The immensely modest Dinezon neglected to provide in his autobiography the details which he related by other means. "Dinezon," Dubnow states, "told me about writing his first novel as a young man, of which he himself didn't think highly; how he became a *maskil* and joined the little circle of the first Mohilev revolutionaries in the seventies—Axelrod, Horowitz, Shur; how he escaped with them to Berlin, suffered poverty and hunger there, and had to come back to Russia."[29] He had, in other words, the romanticism and idealism characteristic of that era.

Yes, Dinezon was soon disappointed in his first novel "of which he himself didn't think highly." When? When he looked about and saw that others who were the most important to him didn't think well of him. He then became frightened of his own success and decided to remain silent.

* * * * *

[28]*Di Tsukunft* (*The Future*), 1929, p. 624.
[29]*From "Jargon" to Yiddish,* p. 25.

It came as a result of his wanting to show off.

But justifying oneself is often worse than not responding. Jacob Dinezon, seeing how the Hebrew press was silent about his first successful novel, "wanted to show the Jewish Enlightenment world that his taking up writing in Yiddish did not mean that he had cut himself off entirely from Hebrew, the language of the Enlightenment," relates S. L. Tsitron. "And he intended to demonstrate this by writing a long article (printed in the sixth year of *Ha-Shakhar* (*The Dawn*) about 'Habituation and Criticism') in which he, in passing, praised to the heavens Smolensky and Lilienblum, Chaim-Zelig Slonimski, the editor of the Hebrew journal *Ha-Tsefirah* (*The Morning*), and others. He figured that with this article, in which he would be recognized as an outspoken friend and lover of Hebrew, he would be proven a *maskil* and could then quietly and confidently present his Yiddish works without offending his Enlightenment peer group."

But quite unforeseen to Dinezon, the article brought him the opposite results. What's more, his article not only did not make him equal to his friends, the *maskils,* or draw him any closer to them, it actually pushed him farther away. It also pushed him away, at least for a certain period of time, from Yiddish. Because "about Dinezon's article in *Ha-Shakhar* where he refers to a particular Yiddish paper, Smolensky remarked: 'A *maskil* that writes in Yiddish is like two contradictions in one person. Those who believe that one must have some sort of skill to write in this corrupt language are mistaken.'"

The impression these words had on Dinezon can be imagined from what he wrote to S. L. Tsitron: "At that time I was a child of my generation, a *maskil* with Enlightenment notions who arrived at writing Yiddish with a certain sense of fear that what I was doing was a blemish on the honor of the Enlightenment which, as is known, always looked down upon the 'jargon.' In me there always prevailed the folk-instinct, that instinct that is attached to and woven into one's native tongue. Nevertheless, I couldn't free myself from the thought that in writing and publishing my *The Beloved and*

Pleasing, my Enlightenment, as if reawakened, could now serve as the muse for which I fought with such passion against the dark forces while I was a teacher in the Mohilev religious school."

"True," Dinezon concludes, "with his remark he impacted my desire to write in Yiddish, but on the other hand, I retaliated against Smolensky and threw away my Hebrew pen entirely and forever! And as a result, for a long time I went about disoriented."[30]

This was the atmosphere for Yiddish literature in the 1870s. An outstanding *maskil* who sidled over to the language of his people had to be prepared to endure considerable despair and resist not a few temptations.

Jacob Dinezon endured a lot and resisted not a little.

---

[30]S. L. Tsitron, *Three Literary Generations*, Vol. 1, pp. 71-72.

FIVE

EVEN NEGEF, OR A STONE IN THE ROAD, THE FIRST JEWISH FAMILY NOVEL REGARDING THE CONFLICT BETWEEN THE JEWISH ENLIGHTENMENT AND HASIDISM

After thirteen years of keeping silent. — Ripening through sorrow. — Revision of the primitive literary method. — A maternal tone in the telling. — Language development. — The *maskil* can't manage to keep himself from proselytizing. — "Compassion with sense." — The teacher who bears the greatest troubles; the small figure that plays a central role. — Poverty deafens the conscience and riches corrupt. — The rabbinical authority and its interests and intrigues. — Idealized figures: Feyge the servant and the imaginary Rachel and Moshele. — "To tears must I bring them!"

Dinezon kept silent for thirteen years.

Following *The Beloved and Pleasing,* which was written in 1877, Dinezon didn't issue a new novel until 1890. Again published in Vilna, Dinezon also gave this book two titles, one in Hebrew and the other in Yiddish: *Even Negef, or A Stone in the Road.*

Over the course of those thirteen years, Dinezon issued only a sparse number of translations, revisions, articles, and, in particular, he became involved in the discussions about language and Yiddish literature. He wrote stories, but had no desire to see them in print.

During these years, his relationship to Yiddish ripened. On one hand he defended the language against enemy salvos, but on the other hand, he did not yet embrace the aesthetic values in Yiddish literature. It was not yet clear to him what was unquestionable for Mendele Mocher Sforim. Therefore, it led to a clash between Dinezon and Sholem Aleichem.

At this same time, however, he became friends with Isaac Leibush Peretz and Simon Dubnow. These were affiliations which had a deep effect on Dinezon's ensuing creativity and, especially, on his life.

*　*　*　*　*

The unhappiness Dinezon experienced as a result of *The Dark Young Man* opened his eyes. He began to comprehend the weaknesses in his first work. As strongly as he believed that a writer is obligated to listen to his readers and please them, he made himself examine why his first novel was so primitive. The character types were presented as if they were formulaic: black and white, good and bad, righteous and evil.

Between black and white there are, however, many more colors. Even in white itself, just as in black itself, there are numerous shades. Just as goodness has no bounds, evil, too, has its endless possibilities.

Over time, his first novel, therefore, shocked the author himself. And when looking at it today—so many years later—it's not relevant to look at it critically from a modern perspective.

The second novel is already a result of Dinezon's further development. *A Stone in the Road* is incomparably loftier and more developed than the first novel. By now one can sense a folk-writerly quality. The persona gallery is better portrayed. There are no more clumsy contrasts. Granted, the good folks are too good here as well—angels actually. But the bad folks are not such extreme evildoers. And there are even types which are a mix of good and bad, a mix of wisdom and foolishness, as people generally are.

But the most important thing about *A Stone in the Road* is that within it are described not just individuals but entire families.

A Stone in the Road is a family novel from an important period in Jewish life.

*   *   *   *   *

A Stone in the Road is the first Yiddish family novel.

Jacob Dinezon presents several families against the canvas of two movements which divided the Jews in Russia: the *Haskalah* (Jewish Enlightenment) and Hasidism. He shows the tear within the family itself.

Dinezon, with no ambitions for language mastery, did, however, free himself in his second published work from many of the weaknesses which "jargonized" his first novel. There was less barbarism, fewer localisms, and shorter dialogue. The plot was more focused. The character types were clearer and sharper. The maternal tone in the storytelling achieved a clearer form and style.

*   *   *   *   *

Yet, in *A Stone in the Road,* Dinezon the *maskil* couldn't keep himself from overt propaganda. He doesn't rely on the reader to draw his own conclusions, but provides them himself. And he expresses the most comprehensive ideas and moral lessons after having portrayed, over the course of about five hundred pages, idylls and dramas that are both comedic and tragic.

"A poor man," concludes the unfortunate Moshele, "lay with a broken leg next to a stone and moaned bitterly. Around him stood many Jews. Others helped him moan . . . . The unfortunate Jew was soon carried to the poorhouse. . . . Some old Jew took a handkerchief in which he threw in a few guldens and approached everyone else with these words: 'Jews, have mercy, sons of mercy! Give alms for the unfortunate one, poor thing! Give, Jews, so God may bestow you with health and long life!'"

But here you immediately notice that Moshele, the unfortunate youth, tells this story about a Jew who broke his leg only as a parable in order to demonstrate an object lesson:

"We Jews," he says, "are merciful sons of mercy. We don't let a fallen one lie. We give him a hand and help him stand up. We respond to every bitter cry with everything we can. Yet, it seems so many of our unfortunate ones have fallen, more than any other folk which can so pride itself in the term 'merciful sons of mercy' as we can. Why, brothers, is this so? Where does such a sad paradox come from in our lives?"

And he explains the sense of it: "We imagine that the reason for this paradox lies, therein, because the good quality of mercy is for most of us born only after the calamity. First, someone or several people need to break a hand or foot and there has to be heard a heartrending cry in order to awaken our compassion. Then we are truly prepared to do everything to rescue the unfortunate one from his calamity. But how can compassion help when the lost one can no longer be found and the broken one can no longer be made whole? . . . Compassion must also contain sense and wisdom, and unfortunately we lack these! . . . Compassion means to lift up a fallen one and carry him to the poorhouse. Wisdom and sense, however, teach us to make this falling impossible, to use all possible means to prevent falls so we have no need for our compassion! . . . No calamity should occur in the first place!"

Therefore, he makes the appeal: "Dear brothers, why shouldn't we remove the stones in our streets so we no longer trip over them? Stumbling blocks and causes of accidents lie upon our roads. There isn't a day when someone doesn't trip over them!"[31]

A Stone in the Road really does show Jews falling over "stones" and breaking limbs and backs. Moshele is such a lively invalid, and Rukhele also falls victim to one of these particular "stones."

Jacob Dinezon describes the atmosphere in which the Mosheles and Rukheles lived, and he preaches "compassion with sense." "Remove the stones from our streets so that no one trips over them!"

* * * * *

Dinezon introduces quite a few character types.

Reb Leizer is a rich Jew in town: a refined and tolerant modern traditionalist. Rukhele, his daughter, is a tender girl with trembling deference who takes after him. She plays the obedient daughter, even when everything in her calls for protest and revolt. Her mother, Chayele, is an entirely different person. In contrast to her husband, a *maskil* of utmost refinement, she is a devotee of the Hasidic rabbi and can't hide her egotism, and, therefore, advances her plans through hypocritical means. Since her brother-in-law, Reb Leizer's brother, the childless Reb Shloyme, is also a Hasid, the type of Hasid that especially loves to make a toast and do a little dance, she pulls him into her plotting when her husband dies ahead of his time. She uses her brother-in-law to ensnare her tender daughter in her matchmaking.

Dinezon delineates the personalities in *A Stone in the Road*, especially the women. Even today, many readers can become hooked by the novel though it contains quite a bit of small-town naïveté and old-fashioned procrastination.

* * * * *

Portrayed here is the religious schoolteacher, Reb Simon, who causes one misery after another. Ultimately, he is completely innocent. Fundamentally, he is not a bad man, though he savagely beats the rich man's son. Why does he beat him? Because his teaching is not by preference but is a distasteful task. He goes around embittered because he neither has a livelihood nor any enjoyment at home. So he releases his anger on the children in his *cheder* and brutally beats them. Ay, why does their father allow it? Because Rukhele, as much as she doesn't want her brother to study in such an old-fashioned *cheder,* has pity for the poor teacher. Especially because he asks it of her. This luckless Jew who can, thanks to Rukhele, feel himself a true guest in Reb Leizer's home, getting food and respect, manages to send the worst misfortune upon Rukhele. Not out of evil intent, but in search of a means to make a little extra money, he simply undertakes the role of matchmaker. And he attempts to join a wall to a wall—as long as he gets a few coins and can also marry off his own spinster daughter. Livelihood!

In contrast, this teacher, himself a Hasid fond of drinking a toast with sponge cake, can sleep away a midday Sabbath at the home of some rich man where he has tippled a bit too much whiskey, and can always come up with a good-natured answer for everything. Even when his wife yells and he has to escape his own home, he replies to her:

"Because of poverty, she yells; because of pain, she curses. And in truth, isn't she right? Should a poor man have children if he can't even give them some dry bread to fill their bellies or arrange a match for his grown daughters?"[32]

When Rukhele is critical of his *cheder,* declaring that it's filthy and smells bad, he immediately comes up with an excuse and points out only the good aspects of the old-fashioned *cheder.* In other words, he says: "Go talk to a girl! Does she even know what the Torah is obtained with? 'Bread and salt is what you shall eat' and 'water up to a measure shall you drink,' and 'on the ground shall you sleep,' and 'in sorrow shall you dwell,' which means: 'You shall get used to living in sorrow.' . . . So go talk to her and make her understand that, on the contrary, what happens in my *cheder* is even better for the children, for they will learn even more swiftly 'if God wills it, one becomes learned in Torah.'"[33]

Out of this religious schoolteacher, who is superficially a passable little person in the novel, arises a central character—a key to the drama.

Reb Simon doesn't want to do any harm to the gentle Rukhele, yet he causes her the greatest pain. He proposes the match without giving any thought to the lad; the groom is barely in his reckoning. He has in mind only the couple of rubles that will rescue

[32]Ibid., p. 7.
[33]Ibid., pp 9-10.

his household. The teacher becomes, in this manner, the most un-scrupulous person: he causes the girl to be sold as one would sell a cow.

It is poverty that thwarts the teacher's mind and conscience. Poverty is what leads to wrongdoing.

*   *   *   *   *

But just as poverty leads to irresponsibility, so does wealth and money lead to transgressions.

And who in *A Stone in the Road* lets himself be misled by money? The Hasidim—those who appear to be immersed in spiritual unity with God.

Here we see how, still in 1890, Dinezon was governed by the *Haskalah*. It is among the Hasidim that he especially observes how they allow themselves to be led astray by earthly temptations.

Dinezon is far from Linetsky's tendency to flog and tear out strips, far from the bloodthirsty satires about Hasidism. Dinezon describes the Hasidic society in a controlled manner with gentle enmity. Eschewing insults, he doesn't even openly criticize. He is sat-isfied with merely describing how they comport themselves, these Hasidic Jews; how they behave in the rabbi's court, how they agree on matches with their relatives. This relaying of the facts is enough to discern the gentle *maskil*.

The rabbinic governance, the court, the rabbinic family, as Dinezon describes them are, on the surface, enveloped in modesty. But it's enough to look closely at small things in order to notice their smallness. Dinezon portrays the Hasidic environment in its moral downfall.

The first synagogue official, Reb Pinchasl, is a politician who plots in every direction. As soon as Chayale is widowed, he casts his eye on her. He, too, is recently widowed but has no patience to wait. Her wealth tantalizes him. In addition, she's young and beautiful. He talks with everyone to seek their support. He works the court to such an extent for the sake of his own match that not only does

the rabbi involve himself, but even the rabbi's daughters and daughters-in-law throw themselves into the politics of the court. Even on
the matter of marrying off Chayale's daughter, they all get involved,
because on this depends the marriage of the first synagogue official!

We have here, also lightly sketched, the intrigues in the rabbinical family: the clashes among the daughters and the daughters-in-
law. Dinezon describes the reception that the rabbi, blessed be he,
makes in honor of the rich Hasidic woman who brings presents for
everyone. Right from the entrance, one senses the hierarchy and the
quarrels at both the rabbi's table and in the women's section. "Everything is calculated. Honors cost money. Everything is a business
dealing!"

In contrast to the corrupt aristocrats, the idealized characters
stand out. Feyge, the old, loyal, simple servant (a second generation
at the Hasidic court) is a gem of goodness and love passed from one
generation to the next. Even lying on her deathbed, her thoughts
are for the unfortunate Rukhele who loves her cousin Moshele and
who escapes from her father's house exactly when they're celebrating
an agreement over her match with the worthless lad. Rukhele hides
until she breaks down and perishes. Tragically alone does the good
servant die, and tragically alone does the good wealthy daughter die.
If one is that good, it seems, one is tragically alone.

However, the broken Moshele has a noble end.

We recognize Dinezon in Moshele when he calls out after all
his disappointments: "Oh, I believe in the good hearts of my brother
Jews. A Jew can't observe a calamity and not want to help the unfortunate one. A Jew can't hear a bitter cry and be unmoved by the
one who cries out in pain. One must only show Jews those wounds;
one must only bring them to another's field in order for them to
see for themselves how many beloved children there are under the
little hills, like little flowers plucked along the side. . . . To tears must
I bring them! Not only are the gates of heaven open in order to allow entrance to innocent tears, also our hearts do not lock them
out!"[34]

[34]Ibid., pp. 489-90.

In *A Stone in the Road,* as we see, Dinezon had not yet liberated himself entirely from his Enlightenment propaganda and proselytizing.

He also formulated here his literary belief system:

"*To tears must I bring them!*"

Jacob Dinezon sought to improve people through tears. Through tears he also bound his readers to his novel.

SIX

THE ASSOCIATION WITH SHOLEM ALEICHEM AND THE CLASH OVER MENDELE

Zeitgeist. — The blossoming in the 1880s. — "A Letter to the Author." — The fault of the Hebrew writers for the downturn in Yiddish. — The times awakened the "impetus" to create. — Dinezon befriends Sholem Aleichem. — Gretz speaks out against Yiddish and Dinezon's pointed response. — *Yudishe's Folksblat* (*Yiddish Folk Journal*) and its crazy editor Yisroel Levi. — Collected works instead of weekly newspapers. — Popular literature or "Diamonds"? — Jews love tears and sermonizing. — Dinezon's stance against Mendele's writing in Yiddish what is more suited to Hebrew. — *Yudishe Folks Bibliotek* (*Jewish Folk Library*) — The breach with Sholem Aleichem. — Disagreement after disagreement: such was the time. — Dinezon's visibility in Peretz's circle.

Jacob Dinezon's return to the novel in 1890 was not just his own impulse, but a result of the zeitgeist. The blossoming of Yiddish literature in the 1880s banished his disappointment.

It appears that he wrote *A Stone in the Road* years before publishing it. That's what one needs to grasp when one compares this particular novel, printed in Vilna in 1890, with his work *Hershele*, which appeared in Warsaw in 1891. It is inconceivable how such meaningful progress could have occurred for a writer in just one year. Such a swift development was the result of many factors.

* * * * *

51

In the years of his shattering disappointment, Dinezon worked in Petersburg on the *Yudishes Folks-Blat* (*Jewish Folk Journal;* 1881-1889), which initially was a side publication to *Ha-Melitz*, edited by Alexander Tsederboim, and later directed by Yisroel Levin—a tragicomic figure in the history of the Yiddish press. In his own paper, Levin, who wanted to have as his coworkers the most important Yiddish writers, ended up as a psychopath in his war against the Yiddish language.

In this weekly, Dinezon printed in 1885, "A Letter to a Writer," signed with the initials M. M., in which he intimately describes in a series of a dozen entries written in epistolary form how a girl from Mohilev became a victim of her old-fashioned upbringing. The girl suggests her misfortune be described in a novel. Let the whole world know! She knows that novels are read everywhere, and believes that for an event to be known far and wide, it is best to portray it in a novel. But the writer M. M. disagrees:

"You will ask why this is my opinion," the writer begins. "I will explain it to you. Generally, the educated Jew considers it to be an embarrassment to read a novel in jargon (Yiddish), and if he does happen to read it, he considers the jargon writer to be a person without taste or skill (this is how a famous editor once expressed himself in a journal), and because no one has responded to his stupidity until now, it is, therefore, clear that all educated Jewish writers agree with him. Therefore, it's enough for me to have written one book in jargon and let the public know that I am a writer without sense and without talent. Why should I do that a second time? When one can hope for respect, it may be worth trying. But if from the first try one hasn't succeeded, why should I be such a fool and not be satisfied with the first disrespect that I've already received? . . . Yes, the mass public is always on my mind; for it I would withstand disrespect at least ten more times and try for its sake if I were convinced that I could bring it something useful, and that my words would not be uselessly discarded. Unfortunately, I'm always lacking in this area, especially lately as taste has become so corrupted by bad and unacclaimed writers."[35]

For a large measure of this insolence, Dinezon blames, "Our learned Hebrew writers, who want to know nothing about the majority of their millions of brothers and sisters who can't read Hebrew works. . . . They don't remember that the entire public speaks only jargon and also has the right and desire to enjoy a righteous pleasure on Sabbaths and holidays."

His second complaint to the Hebrew writers: Why don't they speak out against all the lowbrow fare that is out to capture the reading public? Accordingly, he describes how he, too, dealt with doubt. "I was truly the first writer," Dinezon confesses, "with a jargonist work that has close to 29 printings, but the indifference that our authorities showed me then impeded my energy, broke my spirit, and stifled the impetus to come out with a new work."[36]

The times awakened Dinezon's slumbering "impetus." The times called writers to create, workers to battle, people with societal pressures to organize themselves, those interested in culture to form a new circle, and new conditions for Jewish life—social, political, and national.

* * * * *

Closely associated with the notion of a renaissance in Yiddish literature was the friendship between Dinezon and Sholem Aleichem.

In 1887, Dinezon thought to issue a periodical. (It was never published.) He was in Warsaw at the time (where he had been visiting his sister since 1885). By way of a letter, he approached Sholem Aleichem in Kiev about working together on the project. It is this letter that begins a rich and abundant correspondence where one

[35]S. L. Tsitron, *The History of the Yiddish Press (From 1863 to 1889)*, Vilna 1923, pp. 144-46.

[36]Ibid., pp. 147-48.

finds many valuable details about the history of Yiddish literature and the press, as well as the characteristics of various writers. Unfortunately, Dinezon's letters have not been published to this day. But we discover a lot about Dinezon from Sholem Aleichem's letters. Firstly, about the friendship that bound them in spite of their clashes. The number of letters that were collected in YIVO's Archive, Number 142, speak clearly (and it turns out their correspondence was much greater).

The first letter, in October 1887, begins with "Mr. Kanig" (in Russian *"Milostivi Nosudar"*), and Sholem Aleichem asks Dinezon: "Write me soon." In January 1888, his salutation is "Dear Mr. Dinezon," and he himself writes several pages because, "with your letter you moved me so much that I have to reply immediately." In August 1888, he begins a letter with "Dear and Best Friend." And exactly a year later, in October 1889, Sholem Aleichem is already referring to him as "Dear Brother." And here and there begin to show up: "darling" and "most loyal," "devoted one," and "dearest that I love."

It's curious that Sholem Aleichem, who had a reputation for exactness, called his friend by lofty names in the early years: "Dinezohn" or "Dineszohn." This can perhaps be explained by what Sholem Aleichem permitted himself to write in his letter of December 1887 from Kiev—ten years after Dinezon captivated the public with his *The Beloved and Pleasing, or the Dark Young Man:* "You know that I have not yet read anything of yours? Send me what you have. Hebrew you write well. If you're writing jargon somewhere, I love you, then you're my brother!"[37] Can one imagine that Sholem Aleichem had not heard of the *Dark Young Man*? Or should this serve as an indication that the author of the *Dark Young Man* didn't interest Sholem Aleichem, but Dinezon, in the intimate way he appeared to him in his letters, was for him the "beloved brother"?

*   *   *   *   *

[37] *YIVO Pages,* Vilna 1931, No. 5: "Sholem Aleichem's Letters to Jacob Dinezon" with an introduction and remarks by Nachman Meizil, p. 390.

In his letters to Sholem Aleichem, Dinezon immediately began to reveal his qualities, which later made his reputation throughout the Yiddish-writing world: his forthrightness, his warmth, his readiness to serve, and his love for the Yiddish language.

Dinezon formulated his principal attitude to Yiddish in his coming out against the historian Gretz. This took place during the early months of his correspondence with Sholem Aleichem. During this same period, Sholem Aleichem convinced Dinezon to travel to Petersburg to meet Yisroel Levi, who invited him to come to work on *Yudishes Folks-Blat* (*Jewish Folk Paper*). Levi already then suffered from his illness of attacking Yiddish (although he drew the greatest writers to work on his weekly paper). But Sholem Aleichem believed that Dinezon could salvage this position for Yiddish literature where expression was being given to the then most important "jargonists."

On this question Sholem Aleichem went as far as begging: "I am, in truth," he wrote to Dinezon at the end of 1887, "crazy for the jargon, but heed this madman who is in this case sincere, openhearted, and devoted to jargon practically unto martyrdom. God willing, you will go, go, go!"[38]

Dinezon didn't go. He couldn't.

But it happened that he came to Kiev, and from this meeting his friendship with Sholem Aleichem took root, especially thanks to the story involving Solomon Skomorovski who printed in *Ha-Melitz* in 1887, No. 278, "Exchange of Letters Between Myself and Dr. Gretz." In it he relates that he, Skomorovski, approached the historian with the question of whether he would allow the translation into Yiddish of his work, *Folk History of the Jews*. Gretz responded to this that "jargon is a great embarrassment for the Jewish folk" and he declined to permit the translation of his work into Yiddish. Gretz also requested that he, Skomorovski, "guard against shaming his history."

This "Exchange of Letters," which was published on the cover page of *Ha-Melitz* as a lead article, angered both Sholem Aleichem

[38]Ibid.

and Dinezon. Unfortunately, we don't know what Dinezon wrote in his letters (which do appear to be preserved, but not yet researched), but Sholem Aleichem's correspondence to Dinezon suffices to get a clear idea of how they both addressed this issue. Sholem Aleichem lampooned what provoked Gretz's stance against Yiddish. He refers to Skomorovski not as he was called, but as "Skomoroshka" or "Skomorovits," and adds a pointed epithet, and then another. Skomorovski's aligning himself with Dr. Gretz gave him the same impression as his announcing in the journal, "Give me a bride with fifty thousand pieces of gold, I'm a doctor!" (By the way, two years later, in 1889, Dr. Skomorovski published a work in Sholem Aleichem's second volume of the *Jewish Folk Library* entitled, "The Crime of Gunta in Uman and the Ukraine").

For insulting Yiddish, however, both Sholem Aleichem and Dinezon sharply criticized Gretz, especially openly in *Jewish Folk-Paper* (No. 2, 1888). "Thank you!" writes Sholem Aleichem to Dinezon on January 18, 1888. "Thank you? Thank you very much for your passionate defense for the wrong against jargon! Here I see for the first time your writing—and I like it and I don't like it: I like it because it's passionate, and I don't like it because it's more German than Yiddish; but I arrived at the excuse: for us in Poland, this is German, and for you in Lithuania, this is Yiddish."[39]

Dinezon's approach to Yiddish in 1888 can already be divined from the title of his polemical article, "Professor Gretz and the Yiddish Jargon, or Who Needs to Be Embarrassed by Whom?" In it, Dinezon sets out to prove that Gretz not only hates Yiddish, but also the Russian Jews—he ignores the Eastern Jews exactly as he ignores their mother tongue.

In 1888, such a public stance in defense of jargon, and furthermore, against the most famous Jewish historian, was in actuality a revolutionary step, especially when done by such an unassuming man like Jacob Dinezon. Not only for Sholem Aleichem did Dinezon become the "dear brother."

---

[39]Ibid., pp. 392-5.

In that same year, 1887, when he established a friendship with Sholem Aleichem through correspondence, *Der hoyz-fraynd* (*The House Friend*) began to appear in Warsaw under the editorship of Mordechai Spector, and Dinezon became a worker on this important yearbook. Sholem Aleichem, who considered Dinezon to be his advisor and trusted friend, confided to him about his own plans to create a surprise with a new type of journal—one with the broad content of books of collected works—intended to appear monthly under the name *Jewish Folk Library,* and requested Dinezon to work on it by submitting articles, translations, or novels, and promising the finest honorarium.

The *Jewish Folk Library* appeared in 1888, and in its first volume the ballad "Monish" was printed in which I. L. Peretz transitioned entirely to Yiddish literature. In the same year, Sholem Aleichem surprised the public with *Shomer's Trial,* and also published his novels *Reb Sender Blank and His Household* and *Stempenyu*, which presented him as the humorist of the style and manner that became classic in Yiddish literature.

Certainly Dinezon couldn't remain on the sidelines with his storytelling talent and continue to believe that the decision he made years ago not to write novels was still correct. Yet the years in which he was cut off were a stormy and fruitful time for Yiddish literature.

Had Dinezon not cut himself off, he likely would have—among the circles of those who eventually set the tone for the new Yiddish literature—joined in the process of modernization, the leader of which was Mendele Mocher Sforim, the oldest of the classical Yiddish writers, who already, prior to the 1890s, was the ripest, most focused, and deeply rooted artist.

The years when Dinezon was disappointed in his novel writing were the most decisive in the fate of Yiddish literature. That fracture probably laid havoc to the many possibilities internal to the novelist Jacob Dinezon.

* * * * *

When Dinezon returned to the novel, with the publication of *A Stone in the Road,* he wrote to Simon Dubnow:

"The simple reader is tired of reading all these works where the old ways are made fun of. . . . You probably know that the greatest attribute that our folks-person admires in a cantor is that his singing makes him weep. What was the Kelmer Maggid famous for if not for his sermons over which his public wept bitterly? . . . I think there is no other folk for whom the 'causer of weeping' is considered so holy and dear than by our folk, because a Jew's entire life is a sea of tears."[40]

Telling a story through tears was evidently for Dinezon not just a zealous need, but also his approach to Yiddish literature. As close as Dinezon was to the newest wordsmiths, and as deep as his own love of the Yiddish language, as a writer he was, even on the eve of 1890, far from the verbal artistry and way of thinking of Mendele Mocher Sforim who provided the highest expression.

Dinezon still belonged to those *maskilim* for whom the essence of literature was the moral lesson, and who often didn't observe or expect aesthetic values or artistic feats. He did not even see the higher functions of the Yiddish language which were beginning to come forth when there was no longer any question of whether the language was a means or an end. Even though he had the courage to emphatically come out against those who insulted Yiddish—Smolensky, Gretz, his two beloveds—he concluded that it was too great a luxury to devote himself to art for art's sake in Yiddish.

Regarding this position he speaks clearly in his autobiography: "Art for art's sake," he states in the process of presenting Dik's opinions about literature, "was not known everywhere even in Europe. For us Jews, it wasn't even heard of from afar."

By way of example, he explains: "A story for the sake of the story itself, even when it's a gem, can be purchased by the wealthy, who are not lacking in anything but gems. Our majority, however,

[40] *From "Jargon" to Yiddish,* p. 28.

is poor, lacking in a shirt on its naked back, a shoe, a dress. . . . Writing books for such as these that are pure gems that shine but at the same time do not cover their nakedness, is not only an excess, but also practically harmful!"

In the process of presenting Dik's opinions, Dinezon might not have realized that he was closer to Dik, who was his elder by forty-eight years, than to Mendele, who was only older by twenty years.

This was the reason for Dinezon's clash over Mendele, the founder of the new Yiddish literature. This was also one of the reasons for his years-long quarrel with Sholem Aleichem.

*   *   *   *   *

The clash came about over Dinezon's handling of "The Yiddish Language and Its Writers." This was an overview about yesterday, today, and a glance toward the future.

"Our Yiddish-German," writes Dinezon in 1887, "has just the opposite fortune than the Hebrew language. Whereas in Hebrew one writes and intends that the books and articles be read only by Hebraists, only for writers and *maskilim* like the author himself, Yiddish-German is exactly the opposite; no writer imagines, whether this way or another way, that for him awaits an honor or a shaming from another writer who will critique him in his book. And in truth, the writer of the Yiddish language reads less in this language than in all others, and I myself have not until now been in this matter better than any other. For this we are simply lacking the information to accurately know which good books appeared in this language in recent years that are worth reading and critiquing."

And in this confession he describes the disappointment he had with the distributors. "So I perceived," he arrives at the conclusion, "that they are beneath the value of critique."

But it was not just their little books that made things worse for him, he writes, because "they are beneath the value of critique." His discontent also conjures up Mendele Mocher Sforim.

"Mr. Abramovitz," Dinezon writes, "won't have any objection to my allowing myself to openly say . . . if his goal was truly to acquaint Jews with their present troubles and sorrows, as one can conclude from reading *The Old Nag*, or to praise them and tell them tearfully their historical martyr story and encourage them to further poverty and suffering for their holy belief, as any discerning reader can tell from *Yudl*, if this was his goal, Mr. Abramovitz, pardon me, worked in vain, for the folk has not evolved enough in its education to understand and learn something from it.

"If both books, *The Old Nag* and *Yudl*, became famous, their fame does not derive from the majority, but only from his friends, the *maskilim* and writers of Hebrew. The folk don't buy these books and don't read them, and similarly when they are read out loud, one in a thousand understands what they're about. And I don't believe that Mr. Abramovitz was so foolish as to think that when he wrote these books that he was writing them for the masses and the masses would understand them.

"Therefore, this question remains: For whom did he write *The Old Nag* and *Yudl* in jargon? I especially observe according to my eyes and feelings that right after his first triumph with *The Meat Tax*, Mr. Abramovitz stopped being earnest in his writing in Yiddish-German and earnest in thinking about the language itself. In all of his latest works, his humor and satire is overmuch and too thickly wrapped in foolish and often useless and humorless satire that hides any drop of moral lesson and knowledge. And when I read his latest Yiddish-German works, for example *The Travels of Benjamin III*, I get the feeling that the author is playing around, making tricks, and insulting and laughing; and is dancing on a wire for his friends and fellow writers while concerning himself little with the folk that use and express themselves in the Yiddish language.

"So I don't know how to explain his concern for jargon and show how he needs it. I don't believe that he should be so pedantic and consider the language as a set language of which every word has its origin and source in the language itself; and he is, regarding the origins and sources, greatly convinced that everything he does not find in them is not holy and not needed and, therefore, writes a pure Yiddish. Just as a Hebraist, a pedant who writes and wants that others write only pure biblical Hebrew, or is from the start a foe of jargon and wants to undermine it by way of displaying its coarseness and corruption so it becomes an embarrassment to proper folk."

"I permit myself," Dinezon concludes, "to make these observations because I respect his talent and knowledge more, countless times more, than any other present-day jargon writer. Perhaps he, as a knower of souls, also recognizes the feeling that his last works aroused in the heart of one who is earnest about his Yiddish writing and desires to give the folk something beautiful and useful."[41]

As we see, Dinezon, who came out as the most modern of modernists in his fanatical support of Yiddish against Gretz, actually appears old-fashioned in his antagonism toward the founder of the new Yiddish literature, Mendele Mocher Sforim.

Therefore, it's no wonder that Sholem Aleichem's *Folk Library*, in a polemical article, made fun of Dinezon's opinions, especially after they were printed in *Der hoyz-fraynd* (*The House Friend*) which had Spector as its editor. At that time, Sholem Aleichem was at odds with Spector over the *Jewish Folk Paper*.

In coming between our classical writers, Dinezon was confused from the onset. He had left one world, but had not yet arrived in the other.

*　*　*　*　*

There were moments during the clash between Dinezon and Sholem Aleichem over Mendele in 1887-1888 that are provocative from the standpoint of Yiddish literature—curious and dissonant.

---

[41] *Der hoyz-fraynd* (*The House Friend*), "Historical-Literary Collection," Warsaw 1887, Book 1, pp. 9-12.

Dinezon defends Yiddish, but doesn't take part in it, as important as it is, because of his justification that Yiddish must create a truly artistic literature at a high intellectual level.

Sholem Aleichem's periodical, therefore, attacks Dinezon for his criticism of using creativity in Yiddish as a profession for the masses, in accordance with "one can best affect the masses only with the fundamental Yiddish language."[42]

Dinezon, who didn't understand why such a great learned man and artist like Mendele wrote in Yiddish when he might have been better off writing in Hebrew, was speaking, however, about Old Yiddish and Old Yiddish literature, emphasizing in this manner that Yiddish language and literature has a tradition of hundreds of years. He is referring, thereby, to Eliahu Bakhur and his *Baba Bukh* (*Book of Baba*).

At the same time, along comes Mendele's most ardent follower, Sholem Aleichem, the critic in the periodical he edits, who bitterly attacks Dinezon for his failure to acknowledge Mendele's role in Yiddish literature, but who doesn't know himself the old tradition of Yiddish and its literature, and, therefore, can't understand the source of Dinezon's assertion that Eliahu Bakhur is the author of *Baba Bukh.*

The dissonances are loud.

Dissonance in that period was a normal phenomenon.

* * * * *

There is also something ambivalent in the relationship between Sholem Aleichem and Dinezon.

Sholem Aleichem writes him a warm letter, but permits himself to say, ten years after Dinezon's *Dark Young Man* was the most-read book of the day, "I have not yet read anything of yours." From

[42]*Jewish Folk Library*, Vol. 1, printed in Berdichev and published in Kiev, 1888. The critique is signed by Rabbi Katsin who has a long critique in Vol. 2 about Mendele's *The Old Nag.*

Dubnow's memoirs we learn, however, that "Sholem Aleichem made fun of the 'Weepy Philosopher.' Dinezon himself told me at that time that Abramovitsh-Mendele, after reading Dinezon's novel, called out, 'Little one, why are you crying! Little crumb, why are you crying?' (A gossipy way of referring to Dinezon's small stature)." Dubnow observes: "Perhaps this witticism was coined by Sholem Aleichem in a conversation with Mendele." And Dubnow adds, "I considered making fun of Dinezon, who wrote his works with heart, as a great transgression."[43]

This carries forward to 1890, when Dinezon published his *A Stone in the Road*, and is likely the reason why the exchange of letters ceased between Sholem Aleichem and Dinezon. This evokes the question: "Is it possible that for ten years Sholem Aleichem and Dinezon did not correspond?"[44] Certainly that's possible.

Sholem Aleichem's first letter of the renewed correspondence is no more than a validation of what Dubnow related. "Between us, as it turns out," Sholem Aleichem begins his letter in 1900, "there ran not a cat but a tomcat. I don't begin to understand why you have distanced yourself from me and hidden all this time." Then, after addressing an array of matters related to Peretz with whom he had sharp exchanges and was in great conflict since "Monish," Sholem Aleichem finally deemed it necessary to express his opinion: "I especially need to tell you that I like your present writing a lot more than the earlier; there were too many tears before. To tell you the truth, I have forty or fifty of your letters which are bound together with the letters of my nearest and dearest friends; in them you thought more highly of me, a lot more!"[45]

That was in 1900, immediately after the publication of Dinezon's *Yosele* (1899), about which Sholem Aleichem writes in this same letter, "I heard that it's a worthy thing." Dubnow also writes

[43] *From "Jargon" to Yiddish*, pp. 29-30.
[44] Nachman Meizel, "Sholem Aleichem's Letters to Jacob Dinezon," in *YIVO Pages*, Vilna, 1932, Vol. 3, No. 4-5, p. 347.
[45] Ibid., p. 347-49.

about this same period: "I showed this new work to Mendele and he also admitted that there was something in it that can move the modern reader."[46]

Let us underscore these words: "He admitted . . ."

Why "admitted"?

* * * * *

This was a result of Dinezon's closeness to I. L. Peretz.

Thanks to Peretz our greatest wordsmiths saw what Dinezon could become. In Peretz's circle, Dinezon became modernized.

What Dinezon's seeking could not find with Sholem Aleichem and Mendele, he found without seeking with Peretz.

[46]*From "Jargon" to Yiddish*, p. 31.

SEVEN

THE NEW APPROACH THROUGH
HERSHELE AND *YOSELE*

Dinezon's rise in Peretz's circle. — Modernized. — Publisher of
Familiar Images which is a curiosity for booksellers. — Co-editor of
Yiddish Library. — Freed of old weaknesses. — Without two titles and
without expression. — *Hershele*, a novel about classes taking shape. —
Brayndele, Mirele, the synagogue official, the informer. — How the
Butcher and the Rebbe seek husbands for their daughters. — The
anonymous public doesn't respond directly. — Holy books that
awaken the youth and youth who have no strength to rebel. — The
prisoner in shackles through lofty windows. — "One God could have
been distressed to observe!" — The proper informant against the old
cheder. — Writerly instead of writing letters. — Drawing near to
Mendele's school. — Material poverty and spiritual poverty in *Yosele*. —
Conclusions instead of foregone conclusions. — The religious teacher's
dialectic and the orphan's sorrow. — Two mothers: the rich Sheyndele
and the honest, despondent Khyene. — Reb Saul *Shokhet* (ritual
slaughterer) and Jonah *Vasertreger* (water carrier): the pigeons. —
Yosele, "A little holy spark for other's sins." — Educational and social
standpoints. — *Yosele*, a classic work in literature and for the school.

As a result of befriending Peretz, Dinezon was elevated. At first
in a literary manner, then socially.

In *Hershele*, published in 1891 in Warsaw, a modernized Dinezon is already evident. The change is marked by 1899 in *Yosele*. In
this work, Dinezon is so radiant that even those snobs who had
derided his over-sentimentalism began to perceive the writer in a

65

different light. And *Yosele* was eventually recognized as a classic work of Yiddish literature that withstands the test of time.

* * * * *

It's interesting that "Monish," Peretz's first literary creation, which was the cause of the painful clash with his editor, Sholem Aleichem, was the visiting card that introduced Peretz to Dinezon. And it is noteworthy that "Monish," which was too modern for the modern Yiddish literary humorist of the late 19th century, was actually a source of inspiration for the old-fashioned Jacob Dinezon.

As Tsitron relates, Peretz sent Dinezon a notebook of short stories from Zamość. When they were read aloud for a circle of writers, everyone was captivated. But when an attempt was made to speak with a publisher, there was no one to deal with. Even without having to pay an honorarium, no one wanted to print the book. Publishers smiled: You call these stories! "A page-long story or a half-page story is like a 'chew and spit out.' This was because they were only bookbinders, dealers in thick, fat-bellied stories à la Shomer (Nahum Meir Shaykovitch)."[47] Therefore, short story writers struggled to find publishers. Dinezon was one of the seekers, and he found one: he printed the stories himself and sent the entire printing to Peretz. This was in 1890. This was Peretz's first book in Yiddish: *Familiar Images From Life*.[48]

This association apparently triggered a correspondence between Dinezon and Peretz. In the first letter (which to this day has not been published or well known) Peretz replied on February 24, 1889 from Zamość, thanking Dinezon for his praise and asking him (in Hebrew): "Is this you, Sir, the author of *The Beloved and Pleasing* and "Go Eat *Kreplach*" (a story by Dinezon published in the same first volume of Sholem Aleichem's 1888 *Jewish Folk Library* where Peretz's

---

[47] *Three Literary Generations,* pp. 93-4.
[48] *Familiar Images of Leon Peretz,* published through J. Dinezon with "Several Words on the Publication." In it were stories which established a world-wide reputation for Peretz, like "The Crazy Beggar," "The Messenger," etc.

"Monish" was printed)?[49] It didn't take long for this correspondence to nurture the sort of friendship and mutual working relationship that is a riddle to the present day. Such contrasting natures from such contrasting writerly traditions, and yet they so quickly hit upon reciprocal ways of working together. They discussed editing and co-publishing anthologies, and, as early as 1891, there appeared the first volume of *Jewish Library*, and the second volume arrived immediately thereafter, in which Dinezon offered his novel *Hershele*, published the same year in a separate issue.

Peretz set the tone and literary structure of the anthologies and identified young writers; Dinezon took responsibility for the financing and communications, served as an adviser, and was the one who carried out their mutual plans. This became the pattern for the remainder of their lives, even when Dinezon's name was not featured.

Peretz, the modernist, captivated Dinezon, the writer of the old ways of life. And this immediately came to be expressed in the novel published in the first years of their friendship.

*   *   *   *   *

In his novel *Hershele*, Dinezon frees himself from the weakness of calling his work by two titles with an "or" in the middle. With two titles he had emphasized that he liked Hebrew, and that first comes the quote from Scriptures and then the Yiddish: *The Beloved and Pleasing, or The Dark Young Man;*[50] *Even Negef, or A Stone in the Road.*[51] With these scriptural quotations derived from the Old Testament, it appeared the author intended that if he's writing in jargon, let it not be considered that this was the most important

---

[49]*Letters and Speeches by I. L. Peretz* with an introduction and commentary by Zalmen Meizil, Vilna 1929, p. 36.
[50]From *Samuel II, 1:23*: "Saul and Jonathan, so beloved and pleasing in their lives, that in their deaths they did not part"—as translated by Yehoash.
[51]From *Isaiah, 8:14*: "And he will be for being made holy, but also for a stumbling block, and for a boulder of temptation for both houses of Israel"—as translated by Yehoash.

thing for him; he was just writing this for the "Jewish masses" and not for his equals.

But Dinezon's novel of 1891 bears just one title: *Hershele.* There is also no motto as a justification.

In *Hershele,* the fundamental mistakes of Dinezon's earlier novels are also diminished. The sentimental style continues, but it's not laid on so thickly or strung out and exaggerated. The dialogues are shorter, the plot more concentrated, the descriptions clearer, and the character types more natural. Also, the language is modernized: Dinezon frees himself of Russifications and Germanisms.

Aside from the character types and personalities, Dinezon imbues *Hershele* with images of daily life. Described for the first time in Yiddish literature is the role of theater in Jewish life. The folk-play, "The Selling of Joseph," put on by a group of yeshiva boys, reveals not only how theater was once performed, but also how the audience reacted. Aside from being a moving description, this is an interesting chapter on a Yiddish theater tradition and a contribution to our cultural history.

* * * * *

If *A Stone in the Road,* set against the canvas of the period, is a family novel that reveals the behind-the-scenes battles between Hasidim and *maskilim* as mirrored within the family, then *Hershele* is a novel arising from class struggle. Had Dinezon not been such a sentimentalist, *Hershele* would be a bitter lament about class injustice.

Brayndele, a wealthy widow, is enormously pleased that her enlightened daughter, the beautiful and gentle Mirele, has a teacher as good as the yeshiva boy Hershele. Yet, she can't imagine that this poor lad would allow himself to think about Mirele as an equal. How can such a mendicant aspire to such an heiress? Though he is her teacher and Brayndele thinks very highly of him, and while he is given board in their home—in the kitchen, alongside the cook—he is only invited to dine with them "like decent folk" thanks to the enlightened Mirele. That is: if one is enlightened, one is more decent. If one can read books by great writers in foreign languages, one is, therefore, capable of being honorable. Here we have the viewpoint of a bygone era regarding education: it's only from ignoramuses and old-fashioned thinking that the greatest injustices arise, and education will "certainly" bring justice to the world.

Mirele's uncle, a synagogue official and rich man, goes even further than Brayndele. Notwithstanding that Hershele's a refined yeshiva boy, it's so impossible for the uncle to even considering allowing the mendicant into his family that he doesn't hesitate to inform on him. As soon as he sees the enforcer in the street, he stops him and immediately imparts "what is needed." Aye, this denunciation creates the greatest threat to the religious school where Hershele is a student, and all the yeshiva boys are arrested. Mirele's uncle is unperturbed. He is the authority with the boorish characteristics of a wealthy man for whom all means are kosher in order to achieve his ends.

There is a different reaction, however, from the general Jewish populace. "During prayers," Dinezon relates, "the religious school churned; one couldn't hear the cantor's words. Mirele's uncle, the synagogue official, pounded on the stand to no avail. The public did not stop talking and aside from the synagogue official himself, no one even responded with an 'amen.'"[52]

The public, in general, is better and more humane. Dinezon, who described people who were convinced that as long as they could read new books the bad folks would become good, also described others who understood that knowledge is not everything. From knowing goodness to wanting to be good is for many a great distance; therefore, of cardinal importance is the spiritual level of people. Conscience and morals are more important than knowledge.

[52]Philadelphia edition of *Morgn-Zshurnal* (*Morning Journal*) (reprinted from stereotypes, without a date), p. 169.

"Hershele," one yeshiva boy says to another, "knows that the books are just to awaken someone who's asleep, but they don't have the power to awaken one's strength or set oneself on one's feet! . . . True, I have knowledge of everything, but I don't know how to do anything! My entire life has no order and my learning is also disordered. I often see myself as being lost in a swamp; someone who sinks deeper by the hour and doesn't have the courage to try his strength at getting himself out. I don't have the strength to pry myself out. Too bad! I will just remain a religious teacher of children, a poor man, a cripple."[53]

In *Hershele,* Dinezon presented the struggle between the idealists and the boors, the dreamers and the corrupted, the poor and the rich, the learned and the ignoramuses.

*   *   *   *   *

In *Hershele,* two types of fathers are overtly contrasted, but regardless of their various qualities, manners, and builds, they share the same interests as all parents who have a daughter to marry off. First is the head of the yeshiva who has a pale little daughter, Rebecca; the second is Boruch the butcher whose daughter is the overgrown and portly Sarah-Feyge.

The butcher and his wife feed Hershele and are certain that the more they feed him the more they have the right to expect him to marry their daughter. They're prepared to give him board for an entire week—with what else can they entice him? And in order to be ensured of the outcome, the butcher arrives at the idea of enlisting the help of the head of the yeshiva to have a talk with Hershele.

So the gentle head of the yeshiva does talk, but in the middle of his speech to Hershele, his young daughter keeps entering the room to serve tea and hand out refreshments, and she positions herself so that Hershele notices her. In the meantime, the head of the yeshiva forgets to speak about the butcher and *his* daughter. Truly a learned man, truly a gentle head of the yeshiva, but a father is a father!

[53]Ibid., p. 119.

Dinezon describes with special pleasure the primitive public and how it comprehends and acts. In describing the performance of "The Selling of Joseph," he says, "Although the public certainly knew that the pit on stage was only a crate without a cover, not only without water but also without scorpions and snakes," many "Oys" of fright were yelled out when the brothers pushed the forlorn Hershele into it. "Even Mirele put her hand over her heart and nearly cried out in pain. . . . Everyone was filled with apprehension."[54]

Dinezon paints a moving scene at the end of the novel as Hershele is being escorted through the village in shackles. Mirele, the romantic girl with the sheen of education, a girl from a small town who could easily fit in a big city salon, looks out through the tall panes at her beloved being brutally wrenched away from her.

Dinezon, the sentimental and sweet novelist, can barely control himself. His last sentence is, therefore: "One God might have been distressed observing this!"[55]

* * * * *

The emotion with which Dinezon finishes off *Hershele*: "One God might have been distressed observing this!" is spread throughout his novel *Yosele*.

Just as he failed to observe in *Hershele* those societal strengths that could battle the persecutions and injustices that were perpetrated against the poor and helpless, Dinezon also fails to observe them in *Yosele*. There might be some intimations: characters with hearts and consciences who allow us to feel that they can't swallow the injustices, but they are passive; at any rate, they don't raise any alarm. "*Yosele,* a quiet, emaciated child, responds to blows with indifference, as if he were already used to getting them."[56]

[54]Ibid., p. 45.
[55]Ibid., p. 179.
[56]*Yosele, Story of a Jewish Life* by Jacob Dinezon, Hebrew Publishing Co. Edition, New York, (No date), p. 4.

Dinezon begins his *Yosele* by describing the education in the *cheder* of the past, how the upstanding teacher did not treat the poor children honorably, while at the same time dreading to touch the rich ones. And he concludes his description with the inequality among adults, where the pedagogy is awful, exactly as it was in the old-fashioned *cheder*.

Dinezon steps forth as the protestor against the old *cheder* and as the protester against class distinctions. This is how many understood him years later.

This is how Dinezon was presented after his death in the battle for the new education and for a just social order.

* * * * *

In *Yosele* we see Dinezon at a higher rung of development than in *Hershele*.

In this work, which was published in Warsaw in 1899, we clearly see Peretz's influence in both language and style. Dinezon draws closer to the style of our classicists: even in the long sentence it's apparent how the writer now seeks brevity and emphasis; he tries to fashion the word and especially the phrase. Instead of writing in a belletristic style, Dinezon begins to write in a more writerly fashion, strengthening himself and taxing himself with the form. He, who was surprised that Mendele wasn't writing in Hebrew rather than Yiddish, attempts to draw closer to Mendele.

"Reb Berl," all the other religious teachers say enviously, "is successful; nothing less than a success. Although he doesn't repeat teachings with his students, he's considered effective; although he hits like everyone and gives lashes as is the custom, he's considered to be good, and an expert in dealing with fearful children. Success comes his way. It's an honor to entrust a child to Reb Berl's *cheder*."[57]

He is not deceitful, this particular religious teacher, and also not a criminal, yet much like a criminal, he does things that suit a liar and

[57]Ibid., p. 3.

abuser of children, especially an impoverished orphan. He has an excuse for everything, a moral, a quotation, and a theory. "In teaching," he says, "there lies a great sense." And where is this sense?

Reb Berl tells Menashe Milner, whose two sons are studying with him for a third semester and still cannot speak Hebrew correctly, "The greater the difficulty with Hebrew, the easier, you'll see, it will go in studying the Pentateuch with Rashi's commentaries. This is, after all, a known thing that is especially true for those great scholars, the sharp minds, who don't know a word of Hebrew. And why do you need another reason? Our Rabbi, may he be well, is a known genius with a keen mind, yet doesn't he say, '*velakhidekh beahava*' instead of '*velikhdekh beahavah*'? And what's the reason, do you think? Simply, because a good mind doesn't bother over a small thing that makes no sense."

In language and in the particulars of construction, *Yosele* is a great leap forward in Dinezon's creativity.

* * * * *

Within the framework of Dinezon's sentimentalism, *Yosele* is the most concentrated work. Here the rhythm is faster, the plot more intense, the descriptions more concise.

He conjures up a town where the sound of sorrow echoes loudly, hovering above the lonely, impoverished Jewish child: "Yosele left for the little Hasidic house of worship. There were no yeshiva boys there; therefore, no holy books either. It was dark with just one little candle burning on a stand. The caretaker, an elderly, half-blind Jew, didn't notice that there was someone there other than himself, and Yosele crept behind the stove and slept like a prince."

This little, foreshortened paragraph is more characteristic of Peretz than Dinezon. But it's enough to read several sentences to recognize Dinezon's sentimentalism, his sweet affection for people, especially suffering ones, and more so, for lonely children.

Yosele is such a child—a victim of society where one slander is stronger than a thousand truths. Here, for example:

"What do you say, little boy?" a Jew asked him.

"A bible!"

"What do you need a bible for?"

"I want to study!"

"Don't you have a religious school?"

"No!"

"Who are you?"

"Yosele."

"Why are you speaking with him?" interjected a yeshiva boy who had come over to the old man. "This is the little thief who was just on trial. I bet he wants to steal a book!"

"True, little boy?" the man asked.

"I don't want to steal anything," Yosele replied. "I want to study the bible. Give me a bible and I'll study."

"Here's a bible. I'll see if you can study and if you really want to. Come, sit down next to me."

And Yosele enthusiastically and with great pleasure studied the bible out loud for the man. The man didn't have to help him out.

"You're a good boy!" the man said. "But, tell me, if you can study so well, why do they call you a thief?"

Yosele didn't respond, but his eyes filled with tears.[58]

These are moving passages from Yiddish literature—moving passages from Jewish life.

* * * * *

In *Yosele,* Dinezon emphasizes the emotional tones.

The themes touch upon the melodramatic moments of a child's life, a forlorn child who is poor and orphaned. And the writer also describes them in melodramatic tones with the delicacy of a gentle person who has an ear more for others than himself.

Yosele, a child harmed in the *cheder* and in life, is a victim of various mistakes and injustices that have mounted up within the

[58]Ibid., p. 90.

society. The child sees how money dominates. The child sees that people rely more on what "is said" than on what they themselves see and comprehend. One judges on the basis of pre-judgments and even the trial is unjust. If suspicion falls on anyone, it's hard to free oneself of it. Greater than the material poverty is the spiritual poverty. Money misleads even naïve and honest people. Habitual morals are like a net that ensnares and prevents escape. People are too lazy to deepen themselves. Judgments are formed based on superficial impressions. Therefore, Yosele can't save himself.

If it did occur once that a few coins were found in Yosele's possession that belonged to the teacher, excuses and explanations are of no help: "A little thief!" The caring mother, Khyene, who faints over this, holds onto Yosele for the teacher to flog him. This is how they want to save him! It's of no help for him to defend himself before the authorities who even try to talk him into thieving.

There are a few exceptions, but really no more than exceptions. Jonah the water carrier, for example, and Reb Saul the butcher, people who can free themselves from the vulgarized establishment moral code that hangs on the purse and the logic of the overstuffed. Jonah appears to be a *lamed-vovnik,* one of the thirty-six saintly ones, the opposite of "Sheyndele, a fat Jewess with a three-fold goiter and a throat full of large pearls." Reb Saul is the opposite of the professional religious scholars and teachers who can mask their falseness and lies. When Yosele's sister, Sarale, tries to throw herself onto the open grave, she is comforted by one of these rare compassionate individuals:

"Enough crying, enough lamenting, my daughter!" says Reb Saul while taking her hand. "Your little brother has died—died, as does a purified, refined soul. Let him have his due. And be comforted by this: that not a boy or some sort of thief is buried here, but a little holy one who from his birth until his death suffered for others' sins, for others' evildoings! . . . May he be a good intervener in heaven for you and all of Israel!"[59]

[59]Ibid., pp. 111-12.

These were not merely pretty words. In contrast to the heart-less, deluded, obtuse, and coarse egotists, these particular Jews stood broken: "A few large tears that had continually gleamed as if frozen in the eyes of the old pious Jew finally loosed and ran freely down his sunken, gaunt cheeks, over his snow-white beard, and fell directly onto the open grave. . . . Looking at Reb Saul, Jonah the water carrier burst into tears, and it took a toll on Reb Saul to quiet him."

"Not understanding Jonah," Dinezon says, however, before the end of the passage, "the public shrugged and responded, ''Drunk, probably.''"

The bashful Jacob Dinezon, representing the ordinary person, wasn't frightened of drawing this conclusion: "The public did not understand!" The water carrier had more humanity than the fine upper crust of the shtetl.

* * * * *

Dinezon, the exalted defender of the impoverished and mis-understood child, inserted into *Yosele* language that years later served as arguments for modern pedagogy, for the secular school, and for free thought:

"For what purpose does one teach a child such rules that his young mind cannot yet grasp?" asks Khyene.[60]

"Useless curses!" says Reb Boruch spitefully. "What, is a shoe-maker not a Jew?"[61]

And Yosele? "Now he sensed, though not clearly, that aside from beatings and hunger, there is something that hurts and tor-ments even more than beatings and hunger, and this is the neglect and injustice done to him because of his impoverishment . . ."[62]

"Yosele hears how the rabbi swears falsely, 'May one swear false-ly?' his heart cries out."[63]

[60]Ibid., p. 11.
[61]Ibid., p. 13.
[62]Ibid., p. 26.
[63]Ibid., p. 30.

"'Compassion is cruelty!' Boruch shouted hoarsely."[64]

"'Don't be afraid, Khyene,' Reb Berl said. 'There's great power in the rod.'"[65]

"'Whoever steals once, steals again!' interjected the rabbi's wife."[66]

"'I told you a long time ago,' Reb Solomon added, 'that a poor man is a thief!'"[67]

The upstanding Jacob Dinezon showed in *Yosele*—as early as 1899!—that in Jewish life arose conflicts that could have exploded any day. And he used a child to demonstrate how far these conflicts had reached, about which society was not yet organized, but for which there were antagonistic sides aplenty.

The sentimental storyteller became an awakener regarding societal and educational sins. All Jewish radical circles that were involved in the idea of building new Jewish schools and especially new institutions, took Dinezon's *Yosele* as witness and testament to the unjust order of society. They derived from it weighty arguments in public trials, and his selected pages became the most beloved reading material in the Jewish schools, and even on holidays, in acted-out scenes and plays.[68]

[64]Ibid., p. 32.
[65]Ibid., p. 35.
[66]Ibid., p. 43.
[67]Ibid., p. 49.
[68]Samuel Glaserman, a dramaturge who was for some years a teacher, made a play out of "Yosele in *Cheder*," publicized in *The Jewish Paper*, Buenos Aires, September 8, 1926.

EIGHT

DINEZON'S ARRANGEMENTS TO RESETTLE IN ARGENTINA WITH I. L. PERETZ

The new rhythm in Dinezon's life. — Between Warsaw and Kiev: without a home. — Dinezon persuades Peretz to settle in the capital of Poland. — The plan to travel to Argentina. — The arrangements with Baron Hirsch's representative, David Feinberg. — With the ICA (Jewish Colonization Association). — The idea of establishing a newspaper in Argentina to protect the immigrants. — Why did nothing come of it? — Dinezon's plan in 1890 and 1892. — The letter to Goldfaden. — The long-established resident who wanted to travel the world. — When Yiddish newspapers ceased being published in Russia, Dinezon and Peretz want to publish a Yiddish newspaper in the young and small Argentina.

In the last decade of the 19th century, in the years when he created his most important novels, *Hershele* and *Yosele*, the placid Jacob Dinezon led an intensive life. For the sentimental romantic who had the reputation for being a bashful person, the horizons of his private life broadened more quickly than those of his social life. By distancing himself from Sholem Aleichem and drawing closer to Peretz, his life achieved another rhythm, fresh problems, new interests, and a more elevated creativity.

In 1889, he began to correspond with Peretz. In 1890, he published *Familiar Images of Leon Peretz*. In 1891, in partnership

with Peretz, he published two volumes of *Jewish Library*, which occupied an important place in the development of Yiddish literature.
And in 1892, they both had in mind to "actually" leave together
for Argentina.

During this time, Dinezon didn't have his own home; he remained a bachelor, and couldn't manage to settle down anywhere.
He traveled from Kiev to Warsaw and from Warsaw to Kiev. But
as a result of befriending Peretz, he obtained a brother in spirit.
Each oriented the other even from afar, and each obeyed the other
more and more.

Although Dinezon couldn't yet decide in which city to reside,
he convinced Peretz to leave his native town of Zamość and resettle
in the capital of Poland. And Peretz "eventually allowed himself to
be persuaded by Dinezon."[69] This was in the beginning of 1890.
Dinezon was then living in Warsaw until 1892.

In these two years, their friendship established deep roots. And,
of course, it was difficult for them to part. Dinezon, however, had
to live in Kiev from 1892 to 1896; their wretched incomes forced
them to be far apart from one another. This was truly so difficult for
them to endure that as soon as they parted, they immediately began
formulating a plan on how to meet again; not just to be together,
but also to work together on a mutual idea. This mutual idea was
Argentina. Together they would resettle in Argentina!

Argentina at that time was on the agenda of Jewish public opinion.[70] Though in Peretz's collected writings there is no larger work
about Argentina, one can accept as certain that the brochure "Argentina" that appeared anonymously in 1891 and drew a sharp
critique in the journal *Voskhod*, was written by Peretz, who revealed

---

[69]Peretz's brother, Jonah Joshua, tells about this in his memoir, in the *NY Forverts*,
April 20, 1930, cited in S. Niger's *Yitzhok Leibush Peretz*, p. 197.
[70]Samuel Rozshanski, "I. L. Peretz's Approach Toward Argentina," in *Argentina IWO-
Writings*, Vol. 1, 1941, pp. 117-136, also in Spanish, as a brochure, "I. L. Peretz y su
inquetud por la Argentina," published by the Committee for Peretz-Celebrations in
1945, appearing in two printings of 1,000 and 5,000 copies.

this in a letter to a fellow townsperson in Zamość.[71] As we don't yet have Dinezon's letters to Peretz in 1892, we must be satisfied at least with a collection of Peretz's letters to Dinezon, which address the plan about moving to Argentina.

That was a time when Dinezon didn't have any livelihood in Kiev, and Peretz had only a partial livelihood in Warsaw. Dinezon was probably the one who suggested the "Argentina plan." Peretz replied to his letters (after describing how badly distributed was the *Jewish Library* and "The Little Books"):

"If you have in Kiev a lot of acquaintances and they want to help you, then they should do one of these two things: either give you letters of recommendation to Mr. Feinberg who is at the helm of the committee in Petersburg asking him to give you a position, or encouraging them to send you to Argentina along with a publisher or a newspaper. For it's very important to have an influence on those who arrive there in order that 'people on the side' not lead them astray."[72]

David Feinberg was Baron Hirsch's man in Russia. He represented the colonizing work in Argentina. Therefore, when Peretz referred to a "position" through Feinberg, the position was also associated with the idea of leaving for Argentina. The ICA (Jewish Colonization Association) was then only a venture preparing to undertake new plans for Argentina. Peretz understood that having "a position" that was associated with the ICA would be of value to Dinezon, especially if the ICA "sends him to Argentina along with a publisher or a newspaper," because Peretz had in mind a great societal goal: "It is after all very important to have an influence on those who come there in order that 'people on the side' not lead them astray."

[71]To David Folk, November 19, 1891. In I. L. Peretz's *Letters and Speeches*, translations and commentary by Nachman Meizel, Kletski Publishers, Vilna, 1929, pp. 50-55.
[72]Ibid., pp. 61-70.

Peretz was talking about "you," Dinezon, that is, but is also referring to himself. "Two paupers are we," he writes in a subsequent letter to Dinezon, "and we help each other, as much as we're able." And he clarifies:

"You say in your letter that I need to make an effort in this matter of Argentina and not you. So believe me, my friend, that I can accomplish nothing. You don't believe me that in a matter that relates to me alone, my own self, I can accomplish nothing and am a helpless person in budging myself. Since childhood I learned to do things for others, and I didn't tend to my own garden and can't tend to it now. Understandably, if you happen to get a position, as I wrote, then we both depart and we work together; I wholeheartedly permit you to speak for the two of us, but don't hope for advice from me, nor any deeds.[73]

What resulted from these arrangements? Why did nothing come from the plans to leave for Argentina? Who was responsible? All these questions remain unanswerable. Perhaps, if Dinezon's letters are found, this will be ascertained. It does have importance. It is especially interesting in relation to the history of the Jewish settlement in Argentina.

*   *   *   *   *

It turns out that Dinezon had the idea even earlier of emigrating. This was at the start of 1890. We know this from Goldfaden's letter to Dinezon from Paris:

"When I read your letter," wrote Abraham Goldfaden on May 12, 1890, "I was frightened at first. I thought that you're leaving already, but when I read further that it will yet take a few months, I was able to relax. What 'breeze might still blow' until then can't be known, and if until then we will still see Paris. You will certainly have to travel through Paris, first of all to visit with us beforehand, which will be very important for you; secondly, from

[73]Ibid., pp. 79-84.

Havre it's closer, and the passage by ship is shorter to America; thirdly, one can manage to obtain a free ticket here."[74]

Regarding this letter, Nachman Meizel observed: "J. Dinezon at that time planned to travel to Argentina. Accompanying him would have been I. L. Peretz."

Here Meizel is certainly making a mistake. Dinezon's decision in 1890 to leave for America was known to be associated with the United States and not with Argentina. And certainly I. L. Peretz had no connection to Dinezon's plan. This can be ascertained through several facts:

Firstly, the beginning of the Jewish settlement in Argentina is considered to be August 14, 1889, when the first group of Jews arrived in Buenos Aires with the ship "Yuezer" bound for agricultural settlements.[75] And secondly, David Feinberg only later became Baron Hirsch's representative in Russia where the ICA received permission from the Tsarist government to work officially in 1893. And there are other moments of not as much note which give the basis for being certain that Dinezon in 1890 couldn't have been thinking of emigrating along with I. L. Peretz, let alone to Argentina. Why would they have needed at that time to establish a Yiddish newspaper in Argentina when there weren't any Jews there yet?

The idea of journeying into the wide world was generally a familiar one for Dinezon, though he lived his entire life in Russia and left only for short periods. But he did do a lot of planning. First, he wanted to travel to Breslov to study to be a *Rabiner* (a rabbi), then he wanted to travel to Vienna to be close to his beloved student; and then in 1892, he considered leaving for Argentina with Peretz with the help of the ICA to publish a Yiddish newspaper for the new immigrants. It wasn't coincidental that Dinezon wrote many pamphlets about distant lands and peoples—he wanted to know them and help others know them as well.

---

[74]"Abraham Goldaden's Letters to Jacob Dinezon," with commentary by Nachman Meizel, in *The Jewish World*, Warsaw 1928, Vol. 4, p. 112.

[75]*Fifty anos de colonizacion judia en la Argentina*, Buenos Aires, 1939, p. 330.

This was a period when in all of Russia no Yiddish newspaper had been published for two years, while in the United States the initiative to produce Yiddish publications had been actively adopted. During this time, Dinezon and Peretz had the ambition to travel to Argentina with the stated objective of publishing a Yiddish newspaper.

Had their plan come to fruition, one can imagine that I. L. Peretz wouldn't have played the colossal role he did for Yiddish literature living in the capital of Poland. Buenos Aires, however, would have undoubtedly played a much greater role in the Jewish world, and especially with regards to Yiddish culture.

There was little that prevented their paths from being entirely different.

The placid Jacob Dinezon, even in stillness and modesty, was amazingly active.

Nine

DID DINEZON PRODUCE LITTLE
IN HIS LATER YEARS?

Not true that after *Yosele* Dinezon didn't produce any important works. — Why was so little published? — Remaining writings, novels, and translations. — New themes, greater breadth. — The person of dignity who doesn't want to fall. — Dinezon's aid to writers and schools. — Thousands of letters, a treasure for the history of Yiddish literature. — Anonymous and hidden deeds in the names of others.

The opinion became widespread that Jacob Dinezon through his friendship with I. L. Peretz became so engaged in community concerns and foreign literary works that he barely had time to devote to his own writing.

In general, Dinezon did not make a living from his pen. Nor was he involved in bookkeeping, nor helping his sister in business, nor was he engaged in collecting announcements for newspapers. Yet the quiet, modest, and private Dinezon was basically an active person.

He loved his writing desk. Writing came easily to him. As busy as he was, he felt the need to express himself on paper. And as bashful as he was—it's likely that he remained a bachelor due to this bashfulness—he nevertheless had a weakness for giving readings of his writings for friends and even for certain writers with whom he was not yet close.

Therefore, the matter is not that simple regarding Dinezon's having published little in his later years. That he wrote is a fact. When he died—August 29, 1919—bundles of unpublished writings were found in his room. Among them were two long novels: *Am Habonim, or The Beautiful Rokhel* with four parts and 750 pages, and *Stories of Every Day* in two parts and 508 pages.[76]

They were first published in Jacob Dinezon's eleven-volume edition which was printed in 1937.

Therefore, if Dinezon ceased to publish in the last years of his life, it was not because he ceased to write. The reasons are various. Rather than with Dinezon, they have to be sought in the background, the times, and the attitude toward Yiddish literature in the 20th century.

* * * * *

There is an accepted idea that *Yosele* is "Dinezon's swan song."

The critic of Yiddish literature who sorted the works and values for our literary history, so warmly acclaimed *Yosele* and spoke so reservedly about his other novels that the impression was formed that only with *Yosele* did Dinezon transcend his time.

In regards to the visibility and popularity with the general reader, the impression was formed that the beloved author of *The Dark Young Man* stopped writing entirely after 1899. If he published any more novels, it must be believed that they only demonstrated Dinezon's writerly downfall.

However, this is not correct. Just as other opinions about Dinezon are not correct.

* * * * *

No, Jacob Dinezon didn't stop at *Yosele*. In the works that were published later in his lifetime, there are more than a few mature pages that are important and characteristic not only of him, but also of his era.

[76]Zalman Reisen, *Lexicon*, Vol. 1, p. 707.

Two of the books, *Falik and His House* and *The Crisis,* speak even more to the hearts of present day readers than *Yosele* because they are thematically more interesting and fresher for our time. They contain artistic moments of both a higher level and especially of greater scope than *Yosele.* The sentimental writer comes across differently in them, not only in the travails of the suffering child, but also in the lives of adults who struggle not to fall.

No, it is not correct that Dinezon produced little in his later years. It is even less true that *Yosele* is "Dinezon's swan song."

* * * * *

Dinezon's creativity should be appreciated not just on the basis of the works that remained unpublished after his death, but also in those that he reworked after their publication because he considered it important to bring to them such changes that resulted from his development and new attitude toward literature.

Dinezon's creativity needs to be observed not only in his own work. He had a hand in the overall Yiddish literary atmosphere. He helped mold the attitude toward the Yiddish language, literature, and culture.

Even his translation of Gretz's *Jewish History* was not merely a translation. It was a manifestation of a will that could only exist in one who had a strong nationalist attitude toward the Yiddish language and Yiddish culture. Gretz had asked that his work not be "desecrated" by translating it into Yiddish. Therefore, Jacob Dinezon intentionally did not heed him and translated it anyway!

The softhearted Dinezon, as we see, was not some "weak character." His socio-cultural work in partnership with I. L. Peretz, and later with others after Peretz's death, especially for the benefit of the children's homes in Warsaw, was a creative endeavor.

Just as his correspondence was a creative endeavor, as were the thousands upon thousands of letters to writers and social activists spread out over different countries. Dinezon expended an enormous amount of energy in helping and stimulating countless Yiddish writers to continue with their work.

Many of Jacob Dinezon's thousands of letters contain sparks of creativity. Some of them are as moving as his stories. They describe people and situations which are interesting in and of themselves. In addition, most of these thousands of letters provide an endless fount of history about Yiddish literature, especially in characterizing a large number of writers and the benefit of their many works.

Instead of revealing his creativity before the people and witnesses, Jacob Dinezon used an ocean of creativity in a hidden manner—behind the names of others. But in his literary activities, he also demonstrated that his creativity did not stop at *Yosele.*

TEN

CHILDHOOD LOVE IN *TWO MOTHERS* AND THE CURSE OF MONEY IN *ALTER*

Life is beautiful, but the rules are no good. — Melodramas over traditions and order. — Where money decides. — Between being and being allowed. — Childhood joy that gets disturbed. — The tearful Dinezon begins to smile. — Meitshik and Becka who are not allowed to be as they are: in love. — Alter, the very young religious teacher who holds his switch like an orchestra conductor's baton. — Money also destroys the Jewish world. — When it comes to marrying in order to keep a *cheder*. — The protest against interfering with love. — "Should a heart be broken, there is no cure!" — Conflicts between eras.

Two Mothers and *Alter* (first published in 1903 in the Petersburg *Friend*) are novels in which Dinezon is closer to his other works of that decade than to his previous sweet compassion for his hero-victims. These novels are less drawn out than *A Stone in the Road,* although the overdone sentimentalism doesn't allow the characters to be seen, just as one can't see well with tears in one's eyes.

In *Two Mothers,* two children are depicted who are raised so tenderly under one roof that they feel like brother and sister, although they have different parents. Everyone sees them as soul mates. In *Alter,* the same thing occurs, but in an opposite way: the boy and the girl for whom a match is being arranged feel from their very first meeting as children and neighbors that they are in love.

In both novels, however, the couples are separated. The separations are different, at different ages, and, of course, with different effects, but the context is the same: life separates those who should be united, because by being together they would bring joy to themselves and others.

In *Two Mothers,* Meitshik and Becka are distanced while still in childhood when the separation can merely leave them with a deep, gnawing yearning, perhaps for their entire lives; but no more than sweet memories and deep yearning. In the other novel, in contrast, the separation between Alter and Khanele leads to a tremendous melodrama. Both lives are broken. Neither will find any happiness during their entire lives because they are prevented from building their happiness together.

But while in *Two Mothers,* Dinezon describes only dear characters who are not responsible for the sufferings of others because they can't prevent what happens, in *Alter* we see a Dinezon who demonstrates that the source of everything evil is—more than bad character—the social order in which money changes people in an instant.

* * * * *

In *Two Mothers,* a misfortune has simply occurred: two mothers go into labor at the same time, but one of them, Minele, doesn't survive. Her child, Rivkele, whose name becomes "Becka," is taken in by Sarale, who has given birth to a boy, Meier, whose name becomes "Meitshik." Sarale intends to raise both children as her own, but the upright ladies of the town get involved and prevent it.

"Feh, Sarale," says the rabbi's wife admonishing her, "I wouldn't have expected it of you! How can it be that she doesn't know who her mother was? Before, you see, this was only a transgression. Her mother, may she rest in peace, was busy enough for her own sake during her heavenly tribunal. When did she have the time to give thought to her little orphaned daughter here in this foolish world? But now she is already purified and is certainly sitting there with our ancestral mothers in Paradise; and now she's thinking and remembering her child, and she's probably very embarrassed that her child calls you 'Mama.'"[77]

As we see, the child is not allowed to exist as a child. No one cares that the child's soul will be prematurely disturbed and unable to find its balance, or repose, or joy, which for the child is like sun, air, and play.

And of course, the child's life is upset even more when her widowed father remarries, brings home a stepmother, and then naturally comes to retrieve his "Beckale." Can one blame him? No. The child, whether harm is intended or not, suddenly loses her little world and her peace of mind because she is a tender soul who Dinezon describes as being sensitive and unable to bear the least untruth. Just like Meitshik, Becka is plunged into sorrow when, because of "societal mores," the two are separated.

"They departed," Dinezon writes "after several difficult days, and Becka already knew that there are two sorts of mothers on earth: a mother that carries and births her child, that nurses, raises, and loves her child like something precious, and never stops being a mother as long as she lives, and remains a mother to her child even after her death, as long as the child lives."

And there's another type of mother, her grandmother explains: "When the first one, the true and devoted mother dies and the father remarries, that is, he acquires a girl or young wife who's a stranger, and he calls his child over and says: 'You should call her mother!' . . . Such a mother, my child—you and all good children shouldn't know from her—is no sort of mother and sometimes she's a lot worse than a stranger . . . A blood enemy is sometimes what such a mother is to the child, and hardly knows herself why the child doesn't deserve to eat, be healthy, and live in the world . . . Such a mother is called 'stepmother' or 'stingmother.'"[78]

Becka is actually the type of child that adapts better than most in this type of situation. But, as Dinezon further describes, "gradually the idea dies in her that she is a child that belongs in this household."

[77] *Two Mothers*, p. 12.
[78] Ibid., pp. 101-104

Yet, here Dinezon is not the writer who inundates the reader with sorrow. On the contrary, from this longing he brings forth a ray of light: the children separate, but a spark of young love is kindled between them.

"When the neighbors looked upon them, they whispered: 'Yes, a bride and groom are growing up here. The engagement documents can be drawn up already. They won't be able to live without one another.' And the neighbors smiled in pleasure."[79]

Two Mothers, which begins with a death scene, ends with smiles and the pleasure of living.

The teary-eyed Dinezon allowed himself a smile.

* * * * *

Life, which results in tragedy, brings joy to the misfortunate in *Two Mothers.* Life itself.

In *Alter,* however, Dinezon reveals how life itself is good, and how a person can be good, but due to needing a livelihood, and as a result of the fatal effects of money, people can be ruined and ruin their own lives.

Alter, a young orphaned lad, wants to assume the leadership of his father's *cheder.* But as long as he has neither a wife nor a beard, the parents won't send him their children. So he becomes a cog in the machine called Jewish life.

Although he doesn't want to be a religious schoolteacher, Alter becomes one because of his father, Reb Oyzer the teacher, who has been ill for a long time and entrusts his son to take care of the *cheder.* "And the children loved him," Dinezon tells us, using a lovely literary analogy and introducing a new pedagogic principle: "because Alter made use of the rod not for hitting, but as a conductor of an orchestra would use his baton."[80]

[79]Ibid., p. 114.
[80]*Alter,* p. 7.

Alter becomes a candidate for getting married, not because he wants a wife, but because without a wife he can't get any students to attend his *cheder*. A teacher needs a beard and a wife.

In spite of this, Alter would prefer to remain a bachelor if not for the matchmaker, Reb Fishl, who needs to make a living. Landing a match is as much of a business venture for him as selling a cat or a turkey. On the other hand, there are those who keep an eye on Alter—his father's trusted neighbors, Reizl and Samuel. They look after his well-being and search for a solution. And a solution for them means Alter getting married and being done with it! Who cares about love? For respectable Jews the main thing is to have a dwelling, raise the children in the ways of the Torah, and bring them to the holy wedding canopy. Isn't that enough?

Yet there is such a thing as money, which also destroys the Jewish world.

The very same Feivl, who at first was very happy to consider a match between his accomplished and beautiful daughter, Khanele, and Alter, does a swift about-face after making a good business deal from which he amasses a thick purse. And after a few more good business deals and establishing an office, he's not even ashamed to ignore Alter when he sees him on the street. When he can't avoid coming face-to-face with him, Feivl rummages around in his purse in a manner that demonstrates to the young man that for him even bills of a hundred rubles are insignificant.

For the sake of money, the scholar Reb Fishl is prepared to manipulate the match in every way possible. He remains silent about Alter's military conscription in the hopes of getting paid. But as Alter doesn't want to yield to this, or can't give him as much as he's asking, Reb Fishl underhandedly ruins the match with the beautiful Khanele and instead palms Alter off on Zlatke's spinster daughter, a woman twice his age whom Alter can't bear to look at.

And good Reizl, even though she prefers Khanele, is upset with Alter when he can't forget her, even though he's engaged to someone else. Reizl wants to know why this is.

"And what if I just can't forget her?" asks Alter, his whole heart for once completely open to Reizl.

"You're a Jew, Alter?" asks Reizl.

"What else am I?" says Alter.

"You're a Jew," explains Reizl, "so you must know even if you don't know! What do I do if I can't fast? Do I not fast in misery anyway on the Ninth of Av and on Yom Kippur?"

"But Reizl," replies Alter fervently as heated sparks from his eyes pierce the pall of his face, "I will fast a hundred times, but I will never forget Khanele!"

"Have you lost your senses?" yells Reizl. "I wish this upon my enemies' heads, on their hands and feet!"[81]

Yet Alter gets married and Khanele gets married—neither with their heart's desire. The only difference is that Khanele makes peace with the tradition and becomes a good mother, even though she can't forget her love; while Alter, the religious schoolteacher, pious as he is, expresses his protest by letting his wife be lonely, though it is essentially not her fault. Why is it her fault that Alter falls off the roof and breaks his leg while gazing at Khanele going by on the street? She is simply a victim through no fault of her own.

There are some people, however, who are, indeed, at fault in this misfortune. Alter knows and says, "Coarse folk, those who aren't smart! A leg, they think, can be broken and hurt. That a heart can be broken and hurt even more, they don't understand at all . . . Stupid people! If a leg breaks, you can bind it and make it whole again. When a heart breaks, there's no doctor and no cure!"[82]

The story of Alter, Dinezon's religious schoolteacher, is a Jewish version of the woes of Goethe's Werther, where aside from love's sorrows, the conflict is between generations and eras.

[81]Ibid., pp. 130-131.
[82]Ibid., p. 202.

ELEVEN

THE OLD HOME AND AMERICA IN
FALIK AND HIS HOUSE
AND *THE CRISIS* OF CITY JEWS

Generations and eras. — Falik, the small-town little person, doesn't
allow himself to be pushed out. — Why not emigrate to America? —
The ambition of the weak against the rising entrepreneur. — "The
desire not to disappear." — Loving the ramshackle house as one would
an old wife. — "For a hat a man doesn't sell his head." —
Immortalized in the old country; in America, swiftly forgotten. —
The folksy Jew with deep, thick roots. — "You're not supposed to
make anyone else needy." — Dinezon, a pioneer of the theme of
"here and there." — Artistic moments in *The Crisis*. — True stories
about the merchant milieu, about card playing, about *shmendriks* who
are embarrassed by their Jewish names, and about grown children who
remain dependent on their fathers. — Hillel Abelman, the refined
merchant who begs for mercy for the fire not to be put out. — Money
displaces honesty. — From tears to a smile and from a smile to irony.

The conflict between generations representing separate eras of
Jewish life is most strongly expressed by Dinezon in his novel *Falik
and His House*.[83] In a fine folksy fashion absent of tricks, three types
of people are portrayed representing three different currents.

Falik, a tailor and mender, can't part with his little town, especially when he sees Shaya Miller's house going up opposite him.

[83]First printing in *Friend* in 1904, reworked before his death by Dinezon himself,
but with the last lines incomplete.

He, the little person, doesn't want to be swallowed up by the entre-preneur for whom the whole world is small. For this reason, he doesn't want to sell his house and settle in the new world with his children who live in America and want him to come there, too. Why? In town he's his own boss, but there—what? The little per-son doesn't want to be displaced, just as the long-settled person doesn't want to be torn from his old home.

Falik tells this to his son who lives in the town and is trying to talk his father into selling the old heap: "You mean, stop being my own boss? . . . As long as I have my own home, I can come to your place when I want and not come if I don't want. But it would be different, my child, and it must be, if I no longer have my own home and would only be able to stay with you. Children never be-come too burdensome for parents; parents, however, become burdens for their children, especially when they require shelter with them."[84]

Falik grasps with his tailor's mind the greatness inherent in building and traveling out into the world and has considerable respect for this, but no less fear. Therefore, he's always drawn to catching a glimpse of Shaya Miller building walls, though he's frightened of the big thing that stands opposite him and will ultimately displace him from his own dwelling. He runs around on the scaffolds when his neighbor isn't there and replies to his wife who questions him:

"You think, Matleh, that tailoring is the only trade? You should know that building walls for a house according to a plan is also a trade, a substantial trade, I tell you. And it makes good sense. And that which makes good sense tends to lure, to make you want to simply see everything and understand it better."[85]

And the more he understands the magnitude of Shaya Miller's accomplishments, how a person grows in wealth, in greatness, in his courage to build, the more Falik, as a little person, wants what

[84] *Falik and His Son,* p. 17.
[85] Ibid., p. 50.

he himself has accomplished not to vanish—to not leave what's his own, however impoverished and small it may be.

"Look, Matleh," he gestures with his hand, "over there, under the roof near the attic window. I still see nails that I hammered in with my own hands when we were both still young and you were about to give birth to our first child."[86]

He lives with memories. The recollections make him feel younger, give him importance, pride; they make him happy with what he has. His wife usually doesn't comprehend it—so he gives her this example to make the matter self-evident even for her: "Imagine, Matleh, if someone comes to visit us here where we sit so old and weak and says: 'Listen, Falik, I'm putting down a million rubles in cash for you here, and you just leave behind for me your old, gloomy Matleh?'"[87]

In old Falik is embodied the self-worth for which a Jew is ready to risk all. "For the sake of a hat missing for his head, a person doesn't sell his head. As long as there's a head, a hat will eventually turn up."[88]

* * * * *

Dinezon was possibly the first of the Yiddish writers in Russia to describe this type of Jew who doesn't want to leave his old home even though he endlessly suffers in it. Why doesn't he want to leave the "here" for the sake of the "there"? Because:

"Here I am—me. Some people know Falik and Falik knows some people here. Here I have my house; indeed with an old, leaking roof, but still my own. Here I take up some space in my city, and even after my death, whoever walks by my tomb at the local cemetery will know that here lies Falik the Tailor who was born in this city, lived here, earned an honest livelihood, and no one will have, God forbid, anything bad to say about me.

[86]Ibid., p. 98.
[87]Ibid., p. 101.
[88]Ibid., p. 103.

"But what will I be in America? A torn-off leaf from some distant tree which a wind carried somewhere to a strange woods among other trees, among greener and younger leaves. Who will I be there? What will be my own there? While alive: a stranger, a wanderer; and dead—lonely, forgotten. In time the wind will cover up my tomb and no one will even know that there once lived a Falik and that Falik died."[89]

These moving lines are witness to Dinezon's intuition, a writer in Russia. In America, in the American Yiddish literature, this became a daily motif. Everywhere there were thousands of Jews like Falik who felt lonely even among their own children. Dinezon was the first to deal with this theme in this manner. He depicted not only the helpless child, but also the old father, just as he depicted the young Alter.

* * * * *

Falik is perhaps the most profound personality in Dinezon's works of prose. In contrast to Shaya Miller, the arrogant merchant who wants to fool the simple tailor by giving him a bit of work and throwing him a compliment so he can wrest away his house and put up a mill, Falik is an honest, folksy Jew, like an old oak tree with deep and thick roots that are difficult to tear out of the ground.

As the roof begins to leak in his house, Falik sees that he has no choice but to leave; but as soon as the sun comes out, it drives away his fear of the storm. He's not even impressed by the fervent little letters from his son in America: "Here it's a free world, a Jew or not a Jew, everyone is a person here equal to all others, and parents who have grown children don't have to fear their old age."[90]

All these gilded joys don't persuade Falik. He holds out against all these beguiling words. And finally he finds a way to wriggle out of his children's plans.

[89]Ibid., pp. 76-77.
[90]Ibid., p. 73.

"Dear Children," he writes, not feeling that he has invented this idea. "If you don't have enough sense or refinement, but clearly write that the reason you're not sending me any money to put a roof on my house is to make me needy and join you along with your mother, I must tell you that one must not make somebody else needy, not a Jewish woman nor a Jewish man, not even your own father. And if in America this is called smart and good, then I'd rather die here in my birthplace as a fool!"[91]

Here we have quite a new version: instead of children coming to their parents with a moral lesson, "One must not make somebody else needy," the father comes with this complaint to his children. Instead of the children teaching their parents the scripture of freedom, the old father teaches, "One must not make somebody else needy!" The old-fashioned, small-town father is more humane than his good and devoted Americanized big-city children.

In *Falik and His House*, Jacob Dinezon is a pioneer of the challenges surrounding emigrating to America—the "here and there" in Yiddish literature.

* * * * *

Dinezon's themes and writerly skills, however, were probably best and most broadly expressed in one of his shortest novels: *The Crisis*. These pages of prose are also the freshest for today's reader.

Published for the first time in book form in 1905, *The Crisis* was written under the shadow of the Russo-Japanese War, which impacted the country's economy. Dinezon describes how Warsaw Jewish manufacturers struggled not to go under. Such is the difficult situation of the honest, respectable merchant Hillel Abelman, whose employees have nothing to do and the days stretch as long as the Diaspora:

"Were the boss not in the store, they would know what to do. Were he not there, they'd play dominoes or checkers, they'd argue,

[91]Ibid., p. 105-106.

they'd tell jokes, in the worst case, for a change they'd crawl under a bundle of fabrics and take a pleasant little nap. Unfortunately, the boss is always in the store these days, and even forgets to go to lunch on time."[92]

Dinezon vividly describes how starved the people are to make money and how artful the dealer is when he wants to arouse a desire to buy. The girl who comes in to get change for a hundred is not thinking about purchasing at all, but the boss and the employees work such tricks to dazzle her with all sorts of samples and courtesies, that she comes back the next day with other customers to make purchases.

"Why don't you rest for a minute?" Abelman's wife asks him.

"'If there's a fire, one shouldn't sleep!' he replies. And what he means is not that, God forbid, a house or a store is burning in town, but that the entire business world is burning, and one must remain watchful at all times, prepared to save oneself before the fire approaches . . . Water must be prepared . . . 'Water,' meaning: cash."[93]

And, if one is a respectable merchant, one must keep up with the fashion. Reb Israel Epstein comes along, the state rabbi's father-in-law, and demands a pledge of money to help the needy who are clamoring on the thresholds of the institution. He can't just manage any old way. Which means:

"God is with you! If you pledge a little, the other guy will also pledge a little. Don't you understand that the little boss looks up to the bigger one?"[94]

* * * * *

Up to the present day, *The Crisis* is considered among the most vivid depictions of the Jewish business world. In reading it, one momentarily forgets that it's about the Warsaw that once was, because it exactly fits any city in the world where there are only Jews.

---

[92] *The Crisis: Stories of Merchant Life,* I. Lidsky Publishers, Warsaw 1905. pp. 3-4.
[93] Ibid., p. 16.
[94] Ibid., p. 24

"Whosever's house you might go to in the evening, whether summer or winter, you'll always find a *minyan*, at least—an assemblage of Jews sitting at a table deeply engrossed in playing cards. They play. Is there an end to the names for this sinfulness? The storekeeper plays, his wife as well, sons and daughters play, sons- and daughters-in-law. Bosses aren't embarrassed to play with their own clerks, and they don't play like during Hanukkah until the Hanukkah candles go out—they're not ashamed to play until well after midnight, and what's the result?"[95]

* * * * *

Hillel Abelman has already had a taste of overeducated children. They finished university, but even after their marriages, they need to stay with their father because they can't make a living. And he's not impressed that they chatter in a strange language, though he's not an old-fashioned man.

Dinezon illustrates through Abelman the new type of Jew who doesn't tolerate being ashamed of his Jewish name. The insurance agent, Tabahov, who altered his name in such a *shmendrik* (silly) fashion, doesn't leave him alone, just as his children who Christianize their names also don't leave him alone. He unburdens himself to his wife:

"That's how it is because the fashion is to be ashamed of one's Jewish name. 'Brocha' is a Jewish name, but it's not enough for them. So they'll turn the name 'Brocha' into 'Bertha.' In Brocha there's a 'b' and an 'r' and in Bertha there's also a 'b' and an 'r.' A letter of a Jewish name is enough. But what do you do to them if they give their child the name 'Stefanida' or even 'Carolina'? Do you think that such names aren't given to Jewish children? Do you even know how to translate Naftal Terentievitsh Tabahov into Yiddish?"

"The devil spit on such a Jew!" she sputters out.

[95]Ibid., pp. 76-77.

"Don't spit, dear wife! How's the saying go: 'If you have children in the cradle, leave other people alone.' You don't know what sorts of little cards your grandchildren will yet have printed."[96]

Dinezon, we see, distances himself from the *maskilim* for whom it was an honor to give themselves names that "sounded good" in the language of their homeland. Dinezon emphasized themes that became familiar to the true nationalistic orientation in Jewish life that went under the symbol of "back to oneself."

* * * * *

Hillel Abelman, who wants to be the respected Jew in all ways, is not someone who battles with others, but he does battle with himself. He doesn't want to fall. He prays for a miracle. And when the good news arouses him from sleep that the street is burning, he clearly sees it as the miracle for how he can remain an honorable man:

"One spark can save him. And sparks are flying like hail from the sky." What does one do, however, if the firefighters smother the sparks? "Now, he thinks, there'll come a spark that will fix everything that the firefighters ruined. And he waits for the wind to turn or a flame to spring up from the corner of the roof to rescue him—rescue him from disgrace, from bankruptcy, perhaps save his very life which is attached to his body by merely a hair of anguish."[97]

Dinezon is delicately effective with lyrical accents and tones arising from the tragicomic scenes that pull on the heartstrings. Abelman watches the firemen pouring buckets of water and he feels as if they're scalding him.

"'Criminals, murderers, what do you want from my life?' his heart shouts to the firefighters. 'What do you care if it burns?' . . . And suddenly it is doused completely. Done! Put out without mercy with his last spark of hope."[98]

[96]Ibid., pp. 122-123.
[97]Ibid., p. 129.
[98]Ibid., p. 128.

If this isn't enough, his wife comes along with her dreams. She literally saw, she tells him, that out of the merit earned by her parents, no evil would occur because they were standing over their fabric store with outstretched hands "and wouldn't permit the fire to approach."

Here Dinezon demonstrated a skill for using an anecdote in such a charming fashion that it appears to have grown out of the plot itself. With Ableman's words, *The Crisis* ends:

"Even if a miracle occurs that could take care of all the troubles, something passed down from the deeds of our ancestors gets all mixed up in it and ruins it."[99]

Dinezon travels from tears to a smile and arrives at irony. *The Crisis* is the irony in which the merchant goes bankrupt against his will—even though he uses all the cleverness he has.

Money, that is, displaces the honesty in people. Let one not be tested by the temptation of money.

After *Yosele,* Jacob Dinezon continued to demonstrate novel phases of his storytelling talent by using new motifs which are important contributions to Yiddish literature.

[99]Ibid., p. 133.

TWELVE

A WONDERFUL EXAMPLE OF FRIENDSHIP

The Dinezon-Peretz romance: A page of literary history. —
Contradictions. — For and against. — The too serious one. —
An object for *kibitzers*. — Various temperaments and worlds:
misnagid and Hasid. — Dinezon the famous one and Peretz the
debutant. — The generous gesture for the first book. — Editors
together, ready to emigrate together. — The contrasting views in
the light of Hirschbein, Mukduni, Leivik, Trunk, Hirshkan,
Kaganovski, Ansky, Meizl, Peretz-Laks, Tsitron, and Nomberg. —
The contradictions of discrepancies and correspondence. — The "passive
one" who attacks. — The "ignored one" that Peretz listens to. —
The miser who doles out "discrete death." — Dinezon, the mother for
young writers, and his conflicts with Peretz. — Like "an old couple." —
Peretz's behavior to Dinezon the writer. — "My inspiration." —
Peretz purchases three burial plots and Dinezon swaps for his wife's
burial place. — The most moving letter about a friend and his
farsightedness. — The concern over legacy and the plan for the
Folk Museum. — The mother and father of Yiddish literature.

The friendship established between Jacob Dinezon and I. L.
Peretz is also an important chapter in Yiddish literature and culture.

It's not clear to everyone. For some the opposite holds true. "In
literary circles the opinion was often given that I. L. Peretz entirely
swallowed Jacob Dinezon," and "the Peretzes made Dinezon into
the housekeeper of their household though this is certainly a mistake."[100] There is also the opinion that "Dinezon's devotion often

---

[100]Peretz Hirschbein, *On the Road of Life*, Memoir, NY 1948, p. 274.

led Peretz astray."[101] And there is the opinion that from all the bevy of friends who came to Peretz's house, Dinezon was the only one close, and aside from Dinezon—no one else!"[102]

In light of all the facts brought to illustrate these opinions, Dinezon's image becomes cloudy. This results certainly from his own nature. The nature of this modest, honorable person who allowed his own self to recede can easily be misunderstood. This is why Dinezon's friendship with Peretz is not well understood, just as his literary endeavors are not well understood. He even became a target of bohemian *kibitzers* for whom a quiet, refined person who didn't play games appears to be old-fashioned and provincial. The "modern" making fun of the humble.

* * * * *

Dinezon hated this sort of mockery in general.

"Peretz never allowed himself the least joke at Dinezon's expense even though Peretz loved to make jokes about people like Dinezon. And none of Peretz's friends during this time permitted any jokes about Dinezon."[103]

Dinezon was very earnest and he encountered the same earnestness in Peretz. This certainly inspired him, because Peretz, even when jesting and using irony, was serious. Peretz would enter into childish rapture exactly because he took everything in plaintively holy earnest. This sort of solemnity heightened Peretz's Hasidic zeal and rabbinic attitude, which the mockery-driven Sholem Aleichem and the ironical David Frishman took as pretense. It was natural, therefore, that for years there was a quarrel and estrangement not just between these two and Peretz, but also with Dinezon who bore a grudge against them. In this Dinezon didn't need to follow after Peretz—just the opposite.

[101]Dr. A. Mukduni, *In Warsaw and Lodz,* Memoir, 1955, Volume 1, p. 143.
[102]S. Ansky, *Collected Writings,* Vol. 2, Memoir, Warsaw 1922, p. 165.
[103]Dr. A. Mukduni, *Memoir,* Vol. 1, p. 142.

What is certain, is that Peretz's intimates who wrote about Dinezon following after his great friend like a helpless, stumbling child are quite exaggerated. There are plenty of episodes in which Peretz depended on Dinezon for his understanding of literary questions.

At the same time, they were from different worlds, different temperaments, different convictions about literature and art. Dinezon was a *misnagid* (opposed to Hasidism), like a typical Jew from Lithuania: enlightened and business-like. In literature—entirely naturalistic.

Peretz was a Hasid, a typical Polish Jew: revolutionary and bohemian. In literature—fundamentally romantic.

Such contrasting natures, and yet they co-existed so wonderfully for a quarter of a century!

* * * * *

Dinezon was four years younger than Peretz, but he lived exactly as long as Peretz: to the age of 63.

And just as Peretz loved to intercede on behalf of young Jewish writers in helping them enter the field of Yiddish literature, Dinezon interceded on behalf of Peretz.

In 1888, when Peretz debuted in Yiddish with "Monish" in Sholem Aleichem's first volume of *Yiddish Folk Library*, he came up against the editor who battered his ballad before printing it. But even that which remained of Peretz in "Monish" under Sholem Aleichem's editorship was enough for Dinezon to become enchanted.

In 1889, Peretz wrote his first letter to Dinezon: short and in a telegraphic style without entreaties.

At that time, those in S. L. Tsitron's circle read Peretz's short *Familiar Images*, which no publisher wanted to publish. Dinezon was enthralled by the stories.

Dinezon is the acknowledged popular and beloved novelist known by kith and kin. Peretz is a beginner in Yiddish. Dinezon is old-fashioned and Peretz is ultramodern. Yet Dinezon decides to publish *Familiar Images* on his own. He also adds an introduction in which he says that "Peretz doesn't write to cater to the coarse taste of the lower class of reader; on the contrary, he wants to refine and improve him."[104] And he sends the entire printing of Peretz's book directly to the author's home! This is in 1890.

This fact alone is enough to impart a picture of Dinezon's personality. Add to this, that even in his best years, Dinezon was not a rich man, and when he did have a few rubles it was due to his bachelor tendencies to be frugal. He lived very modestly in a separate, shabby little room in his sister's house in Warsaw, and didn't even permit himself to spend an extra kopeck. So it's even clearer what it meant for him to self-publish a book by a beginning writer, and furthermore, one with a style and outlook so different from his own.

Through his friendship with Peretz, Dinezon demonstrated that he possessed an instinct and orientation that others with greater pretentions didn't possess. When one sees how Sholem Aleichem and David Frishman sinned against Peretz, and only in later years gave due respect to his worth and work, one understands that Jacob Dinezon was far from being just some follower and imitator.

* * * * *

In 1891, Dinezon and Peretz published two volumes of *Yiddish Library*. Sholem Aleichem, as we know from his letters to Dinezon,[105] was terribly angry at Peretz for publishing an anthology similar to his *Jewish Folk Library* and with a similar name. An intimate of Peretz's said, however, that "Peretz began to publish *Yiddish Library* at Dinezon's initiative."[106] Sholem Aleichem could probably not yet imagine that the quiet Dinezon could accomplish so much on his own.

[104]J. S. (Dr. Jacob Shatski), "An Unfamiliar Introduction to *Peretz's Familiar Images*" in *Pinkas*, 1928, Vol. 1, No. 4, J. S. refers to Dr. A. A. Robak's proof of this.
[105]*YIVO Pages*, Vilna, 1932, No. 4-5, pp. 347-349.
[106]Dr. Gerson Levine, *Peretz, Some Recollections*, Warsaw 1919, p. 61.

In 1892, the plan became real for the friends to emigrate to Argentina. Peretz lived in Warsaw and Dinezon in Kiev. Peretz's letters are therefore the best witnesses to Dinezon's initiatives. Peretz says that he is helpless when he needs to do something for himself—so Dinezon does it for him: speaks, deals, writes, and plans. Peretz authorizes him: "I permit you," he writes, "and wholeheartedly, to speak on both of our behalves."[107]

Nothing handwritten remains by either of them about their working relationship from the later years when Dinezon finally settled in Warsaw. There are only the words of memoir writers who are frequently too close to themselves and too far from those whom they write about.

* * * * *

There were young writers among Peretz's intimates who looked unfavorably upon these "soul mates."

"The friendship between Peretz and Dinezon," one of them even writes, "was not healthy because it was a friendship between two greatly unequal people. The friendship actually degenerated over time into servitude on the part of Dinezon in a pathetic and unnaturally one-sided over-devotion from Dinezon's side. The most uncomfortable for Peretz was Dinezon's not permitting Peretz to serve or please him in return. Dinezon, aside from rolling cigarettes for Peretz, would also write letters for him. He did it with great pleasure. Dinezon was a passionate letter writer. He would write long, sentimental letters to his readers, but his readers passed away and he didn't get any new readers because he practically stopped writing altogether. Dinezon took advantage of the opportunity to write letters for Peretz. But he didn't do any great favors for Yiddish literature; Yiddish literature, instead of getting Peretz's letters, was bequeathed Dinezon's letters." And also, "Peretz was greatly uncomfortable with Dinezon's absolute passivity in questions of literature and art in general."

---

[107] *Letters and Speeches,* p. 81.

Dinezon also "haggled" with Peretz when it came to money, especially for others. "Sometimes a needy writer would borrow a few rubles from Dinezon," but he "would always haggle him down. The requested amount would shrink so much that it had barely any value and the writer was not helped by it at all."[108]

How can one then explain that the same intimate of Peretz later recounts that at a gathering of the "literary society" in Warsaw in 1910 while discussing a planned event, Dinezon asked for mercy: "Don't be misled by Peretz, as, God forbid, a tragedy can occur. Poles will first of all not give the 'philharmonic'; and if they do give, they'll attack the gathering, and God knows what can happen."[109]

And how can one explain that the same intimate relates afterwards that in relation to the performance of the Peretz Hirschbein Troupe in Warsaw "at a gathering of 'friends' at Peretz's home, I had to withstand heavy attacks by the softhearted J. Dinezon, who was far removed from theater and protested that one needs to be gentle to the acting troupe."[110]

Do these facts demonstrate "Dinezon's absolute passivity"?

* * * * *

Another intimate in the constellation of young writers circling Peretz relates: "It was often asked in literary circles: 'How would I. L. Peretz's life have gone if the practical Jacob Dinezon had not materialized on his path?' . . . If I. L. Peretz needed some dozen rubles from somewhere in order to help some young needy writer, he entrusted Dinezon with the secret. Often Jacob Dinezon gave it to I. L. Peretz from his own pocket. Dinezon favored 'hidden deeds.'"[111]

This is how one writer contradicts the other.

[108]Dr. A. Mukduni, *Memoir*, Vol. 1, pp. 139-43.
[109]Ibid., Vol. 2, p. 197.
[110]Ibid., p. 218.
[111]Peretz Hirschbein, *On the Path of Life*, pp. 275-277.

Another of this constellation of gifted writers recounts that "everything that came out of Peretz's pen was in Dinezon's eyes pure gold."[112] And another states: "Peretz always shares with Dinezon his literary plans and themes, but if Dinezon attempts to offer a critical word—Peretz always puts him off: 'What do you understand, Yankl?'"[113]

It's therefore worth confronting these two opinions with something told by a close friend of Peretz's and a partner of many years in his cultural society ventures:

"Peretz read out loud the first chapter of a novel—he wanted utmost to write a great novel. The chapter was written very beautifully, but it was already a thing in its entirety, just as Peretz the storyteller was used to writing; there was hardly anything left to develop. Dinezon made comments on it.

"'Listen,' Dinezon told him, 'in the first chapter there's already the pining groom, the pining bride, and another young man who loves her. There are even parents of the young folk who are fighting each other. What else can happen here?'

"Peretz regarded him thoughtfully and said, 'Dinezon, you are correct.' He opened his desk drawer and threw in the manuscript. He never spoke about the novel again."[114]

With respect to the assertion that "if Peretz was too cold to someone, Dinezon's behavior to them was also cold," it's worth recounting an episode in which Peretz hastily dissuaded a beginner from the writerly life: "After several lines, Peretz stopped him: 'Enough! You don't have any talent.'

"The young man was slaughtered. But always in such moments, old Jacob Dinezon was on the sidelines, and with little childlike steps he quietly approached the slaughtered one and said in a hushed voice, 'Go home, write something else. Maybe it'll be better.'

[112]I. I. Trunk, *Poland*, Book 5, *Peretz,* New York 1949, p. 69.
[113]Tzvi Hirshkan, *Under One Roof,* Warsaw 1931, *The Peretz-Dinezon Romance*, p. 50.
[114]Dr. Gershon Levine, *Peretz*, pp. 44-45.

"Then Peretz would speak up and argue with Dinezon: 'One shouldn't be mild in these cases. They need to be cut off in one stroke. Otherwise, you ruin that person's life. With literature, beginners shouldn't be mothered, but fathered. A mother covers up the bad ways of the child and thinks she's doing it a favor.'"[115]

Dinezon, as we see, didn't just trot along behind Peretz. As much as he loved Peretz, Dinezon remained Dinezon—the mother.

* * * * *

"There is a folk saying about the highest form of friendship and love between two people: 'One soul in two bodies.' Regarding Peretz and Dinezon the same saying could be given in reverse: 'Two souls in one body.' . . . Such an intimate bond exists only with an old couple."[116]

Peretz's affection for Dinezon is evident even in his letters. Peretz was lazy about writing letters. And if he did write, he would forget to send them off. But there was one person he was not lazy about writing, even when parted from him for just a few days, and this person was Dinezon. It was to him that he wrote the greatest number of letters, postcards in rhyme, and witticisms; about ninety of these have been collected. Had Dinezon not kept up his correspondence with publishing houses, writers, and institutions, without a doubt we would have fewer of Peretz's accomplishments in all the fields that he plowed. Behind the fiery Peretz stood the quiet, organized Dinezon who didn't permit many opportunities to be lost, who calmed him after his storms, and, like one who sees without being seen, assisted wherever and however he could.

When Peretz doesn't want to have any personal relationship with Sholem Aleichem, Dinezon does it for him. Young writers can't make it through another day, and yet Peretz encourages them to remain in Warsaw. But how? Dinezon responds to this "query" and

[115]Ephraim Kaganovski, *Yiddish Writers at Home*, Lodz, 1949, p. 13.
[116]S. Ansky, *Memoir*, Vol. 10, pp. 164-165.

often Peretz gets the credit. Peretz is impulsive and drives away such and such a beginner; then Dinezon stands up for him and befriends him.

From the beginning, Dinezon saw that Peretz was the greater writer who was more competent and a master wordsmith with the sway of a leader. So Dinezon passes along all the honors to Peretz.

"He carried on quiet 'love affairs' with an array of Yiddish writers, but his true and constant love with whom he lived for dozens of years was Peretz."[117]

"One evening Peretz said to him, 'Dinezon, how would I live without you?' Dinezon smiled in pleasure. And in contrast to Peretz, who was in his lifestyle free and always looking for change, Dinezon was backward and faithful to the old traditions. Peretz in this respect didn't adhere to Dinezon and would often make easy fun of him."[118]

Dinezon also managed all kinds of wonders for the security of Peretz in his old age. Along with Mrs. Peretz, he often solved many material issues. When he saw how his exalted friend was beginning to have trouble breathing and was clutching at his heart, Dinezon arranged with Peretz's wife to have them move to an airier apartment far from the Jewish neighborhood, which led to Peretz's house no longer being the daily address for Jewish writers, artists, and cultural activists.

When the First World War broke out, Dinezon tried to escape from Warsaw without Peretz (because Peretz didn't want to leave). But after a little while he came back; he couldn't be without him.

This quotation from *The Beloved and Pleasing* was often cited about them: "One could not survive without the other."

* * * * *

[117]Nachman Meizel, *Isaac Leibush Peretz and His Generation of Writers,* NY, 1951, p. 255.
[118]R. Peretz-Laks, *Around Peretz,* Warsaw 1935, p. 61 and p. 66.

And those memoirists are wrong who describe Dinezon only as Peretz's "housekeeper," especially when they add: "It was unheard of for Peretz to ever speak about Dinezon's oeuvres; in actuality he did not hold them in high regard."[119]

Certainly Peretz had quite a different attitude toward literature. But what Peretz in Warsaw writes to Dinezon in Kiev at the end of 1893 is enough to make one tremble:

"Why don't you write anything?" he complains, then assails him with "You hide yourself and your voice, and you have cut off the flow of your pen and stand at a distance. I can't understand your ways and your deeds, what happened to you? Can a woman forget her child? Have you thrown literature behind you? Write and tell me what this means."[120]

There were years when Yiddish writers from Russia were sought to collaborate on North American projects with the offer of decent honorariums. Peretz tells this to Dinezon in order to arouse in him the desire to collaborate on American publications. And Peretz writes in 1903: "It's hard to imagine a Jewish reader who doesn't know Dinezon's things."[121] But Dinezon keeps to his old theory: it's hard to break the habit of writing, but not of publishing. In time he also broke the habit of giving readings of his own works, and even stopped telling people if he was writing anything at all. And yet, after his death, a half dozen manuscripts for new books were found.

He freed himself from seeking to publish.

He was someone who preferred to remain invisible.

* * * * *

Here is a characteristic episode in which Peretz visited a city with Dinezon accompanying him. After Peretz's lecture, the local

[119]I. I. Trunk, *Peretz*, p. 69.
[120]*Letters and Speeches*, p. 86.
[121]*Literature and Life*, p. 136.

writers prepared a banquet at which they lauded Peretz with speeches. Dinezon was not remembered by anyone. Therefore, Peretz, in his response and thanks, points out to the speakers that they forgot to mention an important thing: his *inspiration*.

"Everyone present looked at Peretz in astonishment.

"'My holy soul is this one—this one,' said Peretz and pointed to Dinezon.

"Dinezon, the most humble, couldn't bear this, so he stood up and called out: 'No, no, friends! Don't believe him; the inspiration is he, he, he himself; not me in any form.'"[122]

* * * * *

Therefore, it may be surprising what an intimate, a prominent man of Yiddish letters wrote: "Then Dinezon died. It was enough that some weepy little person who hung around with a lot of famous names declared: 'He should be buried near Peretz,' and no one objected."[123]

This story about "some weepy little person" appears strange because no one other than Peretz's relative who lived for a number of years in his house recounts that "Peretz had purchased plots for three tombs—for himself, his wife, and Dinezon" and that "Dinezon, before his death, asked Mrs. Peretz to change places with him so that he could lie closer to Peretz," and "Mrs. Peretz agreed."[124]

The emotional letter that Dinezon wrote to Ansky right after Peretz's death is typical, calling him, "Dearest, most beloved, and after our blessed Peretz, my one and only remaining friend. . . .

"I'm ashamed that I continue to live. But my life would truly be a disgrace if I were as bad as all the others and believed as they do that Peretz, both of ours, and especially my Peretz, really died! I can't begin to believe this. When I stand next to his grave, he is alive at

[122]S. L. Tsitron, *Three Literary Generations,* Vol. 1, p. 104.
[123]H. D. Nomberg, *I. L. Peretz,* Vol. A, 1946, p. 78.
[124]R. Peretz-Laks, *Around Peretz,* p. 68.

my side and reads along with me the little temporary grave marker. And as a hot tear seeps from my eye he notices it right away, and with his reassuring smile he laughs at me for having a woman's tendency to weep so easily. 'Nu, why are you crying?' he asks. 'What do these few words on the grave marker tell you? Silly man, they were written by your gravedigger who doesn't know about life and death any more than a dead man! For him perhaps Isaac Leibush Peretz died. For you, however, he is still alive!'"[125]

And Dinezon, as aggrieved as he was, without hesitation immediately assumed the two pressing assignments which Peretz's death brought about: One, "Peretz has a son. But not only a son, an inheritor to whom belongs all the rights to everything that remains of his illustrious father, whom he, the inheritor, didn't know and didn't want to understand and know in his life, and even less now after his death." Two, "Is it not possible to have Peretz's workroom with everything in it that he loved and held dear be purchased by the Jewish Folk Museum wherever it gets established, whether in Petersburg or in Vilna? Peretz's workroom, in which he created so many beautiful and noble treasures for the Jewish people, working so devotedly and truly for Yiddish literature, I want it to remain in the ownership of the people."[126]

Jacob Dinezon was not accidentally I. L. Peretz's lifelong friend. He helped him achieve his prominence as an artist and his place in Yiddish literature. Therefore, just as in his life, Dinezon also found himself after his death beside his friend in the "Peretz Mausoleum."

Peretz, the father of Yiddish literature; Dinezon, the mother.

[125]*Life*, Redi Moshe Shalit, Vilna, 1920, No. 3-4.
[126]Ibid.

THIRTEEN

THE CO-FOUNDER OF CHILDREN'S HOMES—FOR HIS HEROES

Dinezon: the mother of the Jewish folk school. — The curator of the first children's homes in Warsaw. — "A Surprise." — Treasurer of compassion and love for the Jewish child. — Nomberg, Patt, Mendelson, and Kasden about Dinezon's school endeavors. — The storyteller who ceded the greatest position for orphans. — From his own experience in the *cheder*. — The child was entirely orphaned. — The letter to the Jewish National Worker's Union in 1913. — Dinezon, the pioneer of Yiddishist schools, the foundation of "ZISHO." — The scandal of the $20,000 that Farbstein hid from Dinezon. — "My children's homes and schools." — Why Dinezon did not allow the first children's home to be named after Peretz. — An expert about teachers and a child among children.

Jacob Dinezon, just as he played the role of the mother in Yiddish literature, also played the role of the mother in the Jewish folk schools.

This quiet, unassuming, outwardly passive person, who was the initiator of a great number of important works that hold a place in the history of Yiddish literature, especially with regards to I. L. Peretz, was also a pioneer with the courage to stand up for the first Jewish children's homes in Poland. From these arose the network of Jewish secular schools organized after the First World War under the name "ZISHO."

There were those who didn't believe their eyes when they saw Dinezon at his new work begun in partnership with Peretz, but with which he resolutely stayed and directed in the last years of his life. "If someone had prophesied before the War," one of his close associates conceded, "that there would come a time when the quiet-loving and quietly-loving Jacob Dinezon would become a public person, a curator of a network of schools, a fighter for a matter of the people—he would have been laughed at. Dinezon himself would have smiled. And then the War came and Dinezon became a father of around a thousand little children, a representative of a certain system, a fighter for the Jewish folk school.

"Unexpected, he took on the role. In the difficult, bitter days when the flood of homeless reached Warsaw and the first Jewish children's home and folk school was established, Peretz took him by the hand and said: 'Dinezon, be a curator!' And Dinezon must have sensed this as more than a 'whim' of the great Yiddish writer. And the Dinezon-schools became an embodiment of an idea. And Jacob Dinezon, in his old age, became a partisan, and the first of the partisans. In the history of the battle for the Jewish folk school, Dinezon's name will figure among the first and most active. In his new role, Jacob Dinezon was for himself and for us all, truly a surprise."[127]

For others organically involved with the Jewish schools in Poland, it was, however, not such a "surprise" that Dinezon was among the first builders of the new school system necessitated by the bitter deprivations of the War. On the contrary, "it is interesting and important that I. L. Peretz was selected as director of the first Jewish children's home in Poland, and as treasurer, Jacob Dinezon. They both became school activists, organizers, and fund-raisers. Jacob Dinezon, the writer of *Yosele*—the book of the plight of the orphaned Jewish child, the book of compassion and love—was the treasurer."[128]

---

[127]H. D. Nomberg, *People and Work*, Warsaw 1930, pp. 69-71; *Jewish Education, World Center for the Jewish School at the International Congress of Jewish Culture*, No. 3, NY 1950.
[128]Jacob Patt, "I. L. Peretz and the Jewish School," in *Pages for* [Translator's note: remainder of reference is missing in the original].

And truly, through the first Jewish children's home and folk school, Jacob Dinezon gave value to compassion and love for the orphaned Jewish child.

Who else but Jacob Dinezon portrayed with so much heart the forlorn Jewish child in his novels and stories?

* * * * *

In Yiddish literature there is no other Jewish storyteller who portrays in his novels and novellas so many orphans, stepchildren, and so many evil stepmothers and stepfathers. *The Dark Young Man* makes life miserable for his sister-in-law Rosa who loves the orphan Joseph. In *A Stone in the Road*, there are the hero-victims: orphans like Moshele and Rokhele. In *Hershele,* Mirele is first of all an orphan. In *Yosele,* the child is an orphan even before his father dies. In *Two Mothers,* Becka is an orphan right from birth. *Alter* is the drama of a Jewish boy, an orphan, who becomes a religious schoolteacher because of his father's death. For the same reason he allows himself to be talked into a match. Only because he is an orphan does he not for one moment live his own life.

Dinezon was most likely drawn to portray the drama of orphans because he, too, was orphaned at a very young age. Although he was not really left to the streets, he was immediately taken from his home in Zhager and sent to Mohilev by the Dnieper. That is, he also did not live his life. The child in him ceased to be a child before its time.

And even before he became an orphan, the *cheder* made him feel that a *cheder* boy was like an orphan: "How can one have the heart of a Tatar? Surely of a Tatar, to beat a small child like that!" his father yelled. "But God in your heart? That, you certainly have not! You may be pious, but for such piousness I don't give even a sniff of tobacco! Whoever heard of such a thing, giving a child black and blue marks over his entire little body, and then having the gall to come to the child's father to ask him to let the child continue going to his *cheder,* so the hangman can have someone to keep beating!"[129]

[129]J. D., "Reminiscences," in the *Vilna Yearbook, The Notebook,* 1912, Column 159.

Jacob Dinezon saw the frightening backwardness of the *cheder*, especially along his path as a teacher, instructor, and educator. In the badly organized societal life, the child in the *cheder* was, he observed, accustomed to being neglected like the orphan at home and on the streets.

Dinezon's involvement with the early Jewish children's homes, and later with the first Jewish folk schools, really should not be a "surprise" but a consequence. Rather, it would have been more of "a surprise" had Dinezon not offered assistance and taken the opportunity to help develop Jewish folk schools where the mistakes of the *cheder* and of the unjust Jewish society could be remedied.

As early as 1913, Jacob Dinezon wrote a dedication to the "Jewish National Workers Union" in New York on the publication of a number of books especially for children by I. L. Peretz, Sholem Aleichem, Ansky, Sholem Asch, etc.: "You, children, dear, beautiful Jewish children, you are our future. Be Jews and be proud of your Jewishness! Learn Yiddish and Jewishness, and you will be convinced that you can be proud of yourselves."[130]

* * * * *

It was destined that right at the time of the greatest neglect, the new Jewish folk school should arise. This was at the start of the First World War. "Children's Education" in the three-class folk school, the first school with Yiddish as the pedagogical language in the territory of Poland, flickered out; of seven teachers only one remained.[131] At that time, Warsaw was deluged with homeless children, a portion of them of homeless parents, and other orphans that had lost their parents in the wanderings during the evacuations. That was when the advocates of Jewish education in Yiddish opened, on March 23rd, 1915, the first Jewish children's home (kindergarten), which

[130]Jewish National Workers Union Anthology, 1910-46, NY, p. 370.
[131]C. S. Kasden, *The Story of the Jewish School System in Independent Poland,* Mexico, 1947, p. 21.

became the foundation of the Jewish secular school system in Poland. It became clear over time that "at the cradle of the Jewish secular school there stood on one side the working class, and on the other side, I. L. Peretz and Jacob Dinezon. This coming together was not accidental. On one hand, the school was replete with seething *chutzpah* and an organic connection to socialist and nationalist existence. On the other hand, a noble belief in the life-skills, life-givingness, and 'celebratoriness' of modern Jewish culture."[132]

These are the exact two words: "life-givingness" and "life-skills." Dinezon, precisely like Peretz, believed in this. And while this looked to skeptics like "a surprise," Dinezon not only proved himself with his belief and a holy faith in the life-givingness and life-skills of the Jewish school, but also with the courage to involve himself and do battle. The quiet Dinezon resembled a first-class partisan. "And truly, during the years 1915-1919, Dinezon became the central figure in the efforts for the schools in Warsaw and later also in Poland."[133]

* * * * *

The first children's home was established by dozens of people. In barely a month after the opening, a terrible tragedy struck: Peretz died from a heart attack while he was writing a poem for the children. So the entire effort fell to Dinezon.

"The end of 1915. In Warsaw, three children's homes are already functioning in the Yiddish language. Dinezon is their curator. He tries to obtain the needed means. Himself beloved and welcome in rich Jewish homes, Dinezon pulls these elements into the aid work. But the privation in the city is staggering. Dinezon is truly desperate." So he writes movingly to Sholem Asch for his help in influencing the American organizations to not allow the children's

---

[132]Shlomo Mendelson, *His Life and Works,* NY 1949, "The Jewish School System in Poland", p. 235.
[133]C. S. Kasden, "From *Cheder* and 'Non-Jewish School' to ZISHO (The Russian Jewry in the Struggle for School, Language, Culture)," Mexico, 1956, *Culture and Help,* p. 414

homes to go under. "This is how it fell to the quiet and unassuming Dinezon to become the advocate and the community spokesman for the new school movement. The schools became Yiddish, Yiddishist; the Jewish citizenry couldn't stand them, and Dinezon wound up putting himself in the center of this Jewish battle."

His battle became especially enflamed when the Jewish People's Relief Conference in New York, following Sholem Asch's intervention, immediately agreed to send to Warsaw $20,000 specifically "slated for the Dinezon-schools." But since the leader of the "Relief Union" in Warsaw, Farbstein, to whom the monies arrived, was an opponent of the folk schools, he hid the document and "neither Dinezon, nor any of his children's homes were even told about the entire matter."

At that same time, Dinezon would run to just this leader "to ask, if not beg, for help for the children's homes," but "Farbstein told Dinezon not a word about his children's homes having received monies from America." When the story became known, H. D. Nomberg published a fiery protest article (in *The Warsaw Daily* of February 25, 1916). In New York, labor activists of the "People's Relief" raised the alarm; and since the "Joint" (the Joint Distribution Committee) didn't want to fix the injustice and defend the folk schools, the labor leaders made the first move and disbursed $10,000 that they sent to Warsaw, not to the earlier committee, but to three names that comprised the continuing school committee: Jacob Dinezon (in the name of the Yiddish writers), Vladimir Medem ("Bund") and Israel Reichman ("Labor Zionists"). The first meeting of the committee took place on February 7, 1917 and "Dinezon was voted president and treasurer." The committee would also generally be called the "Dinezon Committee," just as the schools became known as the "Dinezon Schools." And so it remained until July 1921 when the "Central Yiddish School Organization" (ZISHO) was founded.

This was not merely an honor that was given, but a result of his unparalleled devotion. In those years, when he no longer had Peretz nearby, he even quietly stopped writing. "I am in these recent years," he replied to a request to assist in an anthology to memorialize Kadosh A. Vayter, "so far removed from my writing desk that I simply have no time or energy to sit back down at it. My children's homes and schools, and all sorts of other business matters thrust and fallen upon me, take up not only my time, but also my heart and mind, and writing, which I want and still have much to write, I put off for later; later, just as if I am truly certain that I will continue to live and live at least a full one hundred and twenty years."[134]

He couldn't do otherwise: if yes, to devote himself, then he needed to do it with his entire being. He hated the societal "polygamy" of which many are very fond, flying and buzzing around like flies in summer.

*   *   *   *   *

It is interesting that Dinezon, just after his friend's death, was opposed to calling the first children's home by Peretz's name. "As long as its existence is not assured," he argued, "let us leave Peretz in peace. We may not bang on the donation box with Peretz."[135] From such "banging on the donation box," the entire matter would have become clouded. The problem of the folk school would have become an irritation for some people. For others, Peretz would have needed to be more important on his own merit. As dear as the children's homes were to Dinezon, he had no less affection for the idea of perpetuating Peretz's literary legacy by way of a museum that he planned, and he truly wanted to provide for Peretz's widow so that she would not become a burden to anyone and thus, God forbid, diminish the importance of the great writer himself.

Dinezon, the man of compassion, joined his compassion to ideas. "It would be a mistake to think that Dinezon had in mind only the philanthropic side of the children's institutions. In the con-

---

[134]"Life," No. 1, Vilna 1920, *From Dinezon's Last Letters* (written to Mendl Elkin).
[135]C. S. Kasden, "From *Cheder* and 'Non-Jewish Schools' to ZISHO," p. 411.

cern for the child's body, he also remembered about the child's soul and about Peretz's spirit." When Peretz was alive, Dinezon left the programmatic side of things to him. But when his dear friend was no longer, he undertook this work as well.

"Dinezon," writes a prominent school leader and pedagogue, "was knowledgeable about the teachers as well as the textbooks. If a teacher spoke a bad, unnatural Yiddish, not a colloquial Yiddish, Dinezon would greatly insist on this: 'I care not for her pedagogy —let her better speak as her mother spoke. And what's more, the current workbooks are no good. Many of us don't understand that spiritually one mustn't feed the children with garbage! Even a horse needs to be given clean water!' He often played with the children, entering their circle, taking them by the hand, and dancing with them. He remembered the child that was sad the day before, and if today the child was lively again, it was for him truly a celebration."[136]

Jacob Dinezon transferred the sentimentalism and idealism of his novels to the Jewish children's homes where the pioneering experiments were conducted for the modern Jewish folk school, lit through with Peretz's spirit.

[136]Ibid., pp. 416-417.

FOURTEEN

DINEZON THE ESTEEMED
AND THE UNESTEEMED

The mother among our classicists. — The fear of analysis. — Not in
strange merits: where is the balance? — The fate of folk writers. —
"The modern reader." — Everyone wants to be Peretz. —
The embarrassment with folk literature. — Dozens of years of critical
mistreatment of Reisen, Rosenblat, and Segalovitch. — The story of
Axenfeld and Ettinger. — The revision of an error. — Sholem Aleichem
and Dinezon in 1901 and 1913. — S. Niger's sketch for a portrait. —
The ideal folk writer. — Strokes of critical appraisal: Almey, Kenig,
Meizel, Shveyd, Bal-Makhshoves (The Thinker,) Litvakov, Katsizne,
Oislender, Dobrushin, Natish, Krants. — In a difficult environment. —
Medem and Reisen's illuminations: from two extremes. — With faith
in a world of deception. — The blessing of self-esteem.

Jacob Dinezon is, bottom line, the mother among the classicists of Yiddish literature and culture. Generally speaking, without
entering into details, no one discusses that he deserves a place among
our classicists and pioneers of the new Yiddish creativity. If one does
go into detail as to why he deserves this place at the Eastern Wall,
the opposing views about his work and worth can be heard.

Some avoid speaking about his significance for today's reader.
They bring up *The Beloved and Pleasing* and *A Stone in the Road* like
embalmed exhibits of Yiddish literature on the threshold of a renaissance. And the single book that is recommended to read and study
is *Yosele* (especially through school).

Further, come all sorts of merits. It doesn't occur to anyone to remove Dinezon from the Eastern Wall, but mostly not on the merits of his literature. What is added to his value is Peretz's merit, and at other times, the first children's homes, and here and there he is remembered for his loyal service to young writers. "One often has the impression that he doesn't belong to Yiddish literature, but to the Yiddish writers. Rather than being a priest he became a sexton in the 'temple' of the Yiddish word. The modern reader, who can no longer derive any pleasure from reading Dinezon's writings, can still find it useful to study them."[137]

It is, however, high time to pose this question: Is "the modern reader" truly the most important beneficiary? Should the taste and measure of "the modern reader" serve as the taste for and measure of the Yiddish writer? Is it at all a favor for Yiddish literature that "the modern reader" has become the compass and aim?

* * * * *

If one thinks about Jacob Dinezon's life and works, one must consider the problem and fate of Yiddish folk writers in the 20th century.

Folk writing, which at first was considered a blessing for Yiddish literature given before the Torah, began to be considered a "remnant" of the primitive masses of the 19th century, and "the modern reader" became the spoiled child for most contemporary Yiddish writers. Therefore, everyone wanted to be like Peretz.

"The modern reader" became so in fashion and so privileged for the new Yiddish literature, that in focusing on him in order to win him over, the Jewish critics overlooked and nearly ignored many of those literary creations that did not appeal to the snobbery of modern readers.

On this account, Jacob Dinezon became the greatest victim.

[137] S. Niger, "Jacob Dinezon", in *Literary Pages*, Warsaw, October 11, 1929, N. 284.

Our critics, with their masculine bent and mostly with the imprint of Yeshiva-boys, simply became embarrassed with this storyteller due to his great appeal to women. Therefore, the reason shouldn't be sought with Dinezon that his recognition became limited to *Yosele*. The Yiddish literary critics and historians are responsible for this, not Dinezon.

The theory that the high quality of modern Yiddish literature is its best safeguard is, on one hand, a significant feature of its development; on the other hand, this theory leads to the easy disregard for the mass reader and folk literature, thanks to which our writerly skill stood out and was surrounded by the adoration of the masses, although only understood by tiny circles, and often misunderstood.

* * * * *

Our critics, arising on the threshold of the 20th century, became so caught up in the sharpness of language and artistic wizardry, they were often ashamed to look around at true folk writers who captured the hearts of the masses with integrity.

Naturally, the critics didn't intend to harm the folk literature; by overlooking the folk writer they merely intended to improve the lot of the intelligentsia, to elevate the level of Yiddish writerly skill, and to forge a path for literary masters who didn't usually appeal to the masses. This is fair. However, at the same time, one injustice after another was perpetrated against great folk writers.

Jacob Dinezon is not the only one in Yiddish literature who was denigrated by our critics. This affected him so mercilessly that even when he continued to write, he hid his writing—wrote and put it away in his desk drawer. For himself! In Peretz's time, Maeterlinck and Baudelaire were already looked up to.

In this manner, Abraham Reisen was disparaged by our critics for decades. For decades, Zusman Segalovitch was also minimized, though it was known that he was the most-read novelist in Poland.

And even the modern H. Rosenblatt paid dearly for his love of down-home motifs.

With this kind of approach established, it was not relevant to "unearth" and make public the works of the meaningful Yiddish novelist Israel Aksenfeld (1789-1868). And it is truly a wonder that there lived the juicy writer of fables, epigrams, and comedies, Shlomo Ettinger (1803-1856). It may be that he was uncovered and later researched sooner than everyone else thanks to the curiosities of his life and his descendants.

Jacob Dinezon, who for the sake of countless people had elbows to make way for others but never for himself, was unjustly pushed to the side. And if one uses his name in the same breath as the names of our classicists and their grandiose pioneering works, there are those who have the impression that this is not due to his own self but because he forged himself into the golden chain of our initial primary writers.

From this error, which touches upon many names and works, we must free ourselves.

* * * * *

"In my opinion, it turns out," wrote Sholem Aleichem to Dinezon after their reconciliation in 1901, "that you are too honest a man; you should have been born either fifty years earlier or a hundred years later (if we believe that we're going forward ethically). . . .Why are you such a pauper?" In a subsequent letter in 1902, Sholem Aleichem complained: "You are after all something of a pioneer for us, your name is Dinezon, and no two Dinezons does our poor young folk literature have."[138]

This is when Sholem Aleichem wanted to know when it was possible to celebrate Dinezon's birthday and Dinezon didn't want to tell him his secret.

[138] *YIVO Pages,* Vilna 1932, Vol. 3, pp. 350-352.

In 1913, when Sholem Aleichem was very sick, Dinezon wrote to him with warm and loving feelings: "Remember, try as quickly as possible to recover fully." And Dinezon again revealed his "weakness" regarding initiatives: "A plan is about to be born in me. We, that is: you, Peretz, and I, should travel to Israel, look around, and tell about everything that we see there with our own eyes and feel with our hearts, treading on the ground from which we stem, in which are hidden all our spiritual roots, and to which our prayers and hopes are directed. . . . So better be healthy, if only for my and Peretz's sake."[139]

This warm bond is not a pure accident. There was, in this affection, quite a mutual seed and source that kept them together. This particular bond is called Yiddish literature—our soul, our destiny.

* * * * *

It is, therefore, inordinately important and pertinent what S. Niger encapsulated on Dinezon's tenth memorial day: "Jacob Dinezon awaits a skilled writer to describe his innermost portrait. He awaits someone who must not imagine that he can dispatch him with a few bold strokes, or fulfill his duty with a gross line. Dinezon was not at all plain and simple as many believe. He merely appeared that way. Only on the surface was he 'an old child,' as some say with sympathy, or an 'immature person,' as others mock. He was much more than that, though he was also that. Remember: he was a student of Isaac Meier Dik and a friend of Isaac Leibush Peretz—is not this contradiction enough to show that he was not such a straightforward person? Dik and Peretz—these are two different worlds. Dik is the Old World; Peretz the Modern Jewish World. Dik is the folk person, the primitive; Peretz, the intelligentsia, the complexity. How was it possible that the same Jacob Dinezon, who in his writing embodied the Musar elements of the once extant *Haskalah* movement, should, with all his other activities, help to elevate the father of

[139]*All the Works of Sholem Aleichem*, NY 1919, "A Week With I. L. Peretz," p. 73.

modern Yiddish literature? Dinezon was not such an ordinary character as many believe. He was also not such a pauper or Bontshe the Silent as one might have imagined. He was, on the contrary, very ambitious. Here you have a characteristic fact: when the behavior of his readership or the behavior of his writer colleagues did not appeal to him, he, in his unique manner, protested. He stopped publishing his work."[140]

Outwardly, this diminutive little Jew who became prematurely grey, was shrunken, walked quietly "as if in socks," was often bent over by worries, and when he smiled, his smile was helpless; and only when he stood alongside Peretz did the *Shekhinah* rest upon him as upon a mother who is happily gazing upon her wunderkind. Inwardly, there was a healthy folk person of strong character who maintained the healthy inner principles of a refined *maskil* modernized by the nationalist ideals of the early 20th century. He was the ideal folk writer who provided the example of the ideal person. He avoided commercialization. He did not want to put himself in the public eye. Yet he was always prepared to do what was useful for the community in the framework of his writerly interests.

Dinezon, however, like Peretz, did not have a social circle around him. "Always at the center of the self-created Yiddish literature, practically of the entire new Yiddish culture, Peretz was terribly lonely. Peretz didn't have a social circle, didn't sense a foundation under his feet; everything was in chaos, not developed, not organized, ready to be disturbed or to vanish completely."[141]

So what is so surprising about Dinezon being shoved into a corner?

One must remember the great injustice that our literary critics committed and continue to commit regarding the pioneers of the great Yiddish novel, Spector and Dinezon. Dinezon's novels are full of refined, pitiable people: orphans and lonesome ones who evoke

[140] *Jacob Dinezon*, L. B., 1929, No. 284.
[141] S. Ansky, *Memoir*, pp. 165-166.

compassion and tears. Even his villains can barely stand on their own two feet. Who remembers them, these two great writers? Their memorial days are not observed and no one has written a monograph about them. Always these three: Mendele Mocher Sforim, Sholem Aleichem, and I. L. Peretz. These three giants deserve all the monuments in our literature. But Spector and Dinezon certainly deserve not to have so disappeared.[142]

Dinezon had ambition. In several areas he achieved much more than other great and greater writers of his day. When he spoke about creativity in Yiddish, he did not limit himself, as others did, to writers of his setting, but even referred to Eliahu Bakhur and his *Baba Bukh*. As incorrect as he was in 1888, it is acknowledged, "that Dinezon's critique of Mendele is one of the most interesting because it reveals his own thinking and the times in our literature."[143] He already saw Peretz's grandness in the dawn and defended it against Sholem Aleichem's *kibitzing* and David Frishman's mockery.[144]

When they wanted to publish Peretz's collected works for his first celebration, Peretz didn't have them, "but Dinezon tirelessly gathered them, searched for over a year in forgotten Yiddish anthologies, leafed through journals and newspapers with blackened letters, and assembled them line by line, page by page."[145] Only a person with a broad outlook could have, at the start of the 20th century, so widely encompassed values and works. Only with his consciousness, with his ambition and faith, was it possible to be so stubbornly on his own.

"Jacob Dinezon is the optimist in our Yiddish literature. He is practically the sole one who loves the people that he describes in his novels. And he is certain that goodness will always triumph."[146]

[142]A. Almi, *Moments of a Life*, B. A. 1948, pp. 178-179.
[143]Leo Kenig, *Folk and Literature*, London 1947, p. 44.
[144]Nachman Meizel, "Peretz and Sholem Aleichem," in *Philological Writings*, by YIVO, Vilna 1926, Vol. 1, pp. 268-269.
[145]Mark Shveid, *Comfort My Folk*, NY 1955, p. 238.
[146]Bal-Makhshoves (The Thinker), *Selected Writings*, Vol. 1, p. 116.

This is how Dinezon appeared in his novels and stories; this is how he appeared in his thousands upon thousands of letters. "In Jacob Dinezon's creations that crossover the paths that lead from A. M. Dik and Shomer, they shorten the further distance to Mendele and Sholem Aleichem."[147] This path is not shadowed. It is also here today. A number of readers today are seeking the writers on this path, a healthy number, and writers of integrity. And if not any "modern ones"—do we not need them? Must we lose them?

* * * * *

Upon consideration, even the most modernist can arrive at this conclusion: "This frail Dinezon, the softhearted one with a feminine soul—earned the true, the 'most consistent' folk credit. He was the true writer of the people. It was not society that read him, but really the folk. Pious mothers, dreamy daughters, bearded fathers— entire families read him. Mitzkevitch longed for this; Dinezon achieved it.

"Two authentic folk writers were ours: Dinezon and Sholem Aleichem. It doesn't occur to anyone to put these two writers on the same level. Yet it is so: in their main artistic accomplishments they are paradoxically alike. Dinezon is the lachrymose one and Sholem Aleichem is the clown. Both are effective by way of the same theatrical means, both crease the face of the folk and force it to play along. The former to weeping; the latter to laughing.

"Do not dismiss the sentimentality of the art. Authentic sentimentality is as justified as authentic humor. Both methods are primitive effects. You will cry as naturally reading Dinezon as you will naturally burst into laughter with Sholem Aleichem. The folk hate to remain neutral. Could there be a way, a possibility of lobbing the seed of individual higher truth and the seed of art from intuitive sworn writers over the heads of the snobs in limited reading circles directly to the folk?"[148]

[147]M. Litvakov, *In Restlessness,* Vol. 2, Moscow 1926.
[148]Alter Katsizne, "The Problem, Dinezon," in *Literary Pages,* Warsaw 1924, No. 22.

This is not just a mindless question. Winning over the reader is not a small thing. "Some writers . . . turn back to the tendencies and methods of Isaac Meier Dik and Jacob Dinezon. Therefore, may they and their readers once again find use and appeal in the naïve novel?"[149]

*　*　*　*　*

And certainly Dinezon brings a usefulness and appeal to those writers who seek material in literature for social stimulation. *The Dark Young Man* is a typical representation of Mendele's "Knupye" characters. The general reader of the 1870s had the complete right to see in Dinezon's novels a further development of the program from which Mendele's "direction came into the literature. It is therefore no wonder that it was this reader who bestowed upon Dinezon the same sympathy which he, the general reader, demonstrated more than once in relationship to Mendele's works."[150]

Therefore, a revolutionary critic, in breaking with the past, expressed, "The Jewish sentimental literature is, like every sentimental literature, a truly readable, needed evolution of form. . . . The Dinezon opus is saturated with belletristic culture. . . . Dinezon's homey words in the manner of *Tsene Rene,* faithfully mirrored the elementary familial and customary desires of those meaningful reading circles that gave him, seemingly, ready sentimental material."[151] The conclusion: "The Enlightenment conflict which was for such writers like Mendele and Linetski of implacable consequence, was for Dinezon: compromise."[152]

---

[149]S. Niger, "Fifty Years After Jacob Dinezon's 'Dark Young Man,'" in *Di Tsukunft* (*The Future*), NY 1928, No. 5.

[150]N. Oyslender, "Mendele's Accompanists in the 60s and 70s," in *Mendele and His Time,* State publication, *The Truth,* Moscow 1940, p. 115.

[151]I. Zobrushin, "Thoughtway," Kiev 1922, Chapter in *Yiddish Literature,* Kiev 1928, p. 151.

[152]Michael Natish, "Elements of Dinezon's Personality," Introduction to *A Year's Work in Graduate Studies at YIVO,* Vilna 1937, p. 31. Mendl Elkin, Librarian of YIVO in New York informed me (9-11-1956) that among the rescued materials was Natish's manuscript, around 500 pages, "Written on pieces and crumbs of paper."

The compromise was not due to weakness, as many think, but actually because of human determination and thought.

* * * * *

"In the midst of the trivial tumult of life, in the midst of the noisy small literary world that was more full of shouting, more disquieting and ill-mannered than all the rest, he remained tranquil, pure, and genteel. A white dove among the black crows and puffedup false peacocks."[153] This is the characterization of a person who knew Jacob Dinezon for a long time as a daily co-worker and who was not quick to praise. Therefore, it is only natural that an exalted, sentimental person who liked to bestow compliments, in recollecting Dinezon's affectionate correspondence, would say: "Of everything that's good . . . hopes . . . words of comfort . . . clever speech . . . full of good-humored ideas, full of sincere humor . . . Received from Dinezon over a short period of time thirty postcards . . . Some of them I knew by heart . . . He wrote with zeal."[154]

Tens of thousands of letters—doves—sent by Dinezon all over the world. Many of them infused writers and cultural activists with a fresh soul.

"A Jew who knows Hebrew and writes jargon," Dinezon said in 1907 in one of his letters to Philip Krantz, "was sometimes considered worse than a Jew who converted to Christianity," and therefore, "there is one law, one principle in our time: only to be strong."[155]

If it is true what Philip Krantz relates in his series of articles about *The Dark Young Man* that "according to Dinezon's words, this novel sold two hundred thousand copies over several years,"[156] one would've had to be the greatest hero after such a fantastic popu-

[153]V. Medem, *From My Notebook,* Warsaw 1929, p. 129.
[154]Abraham Reisen, *Episodes from My Life,* Vilna 1929, First Part, pp. 29-32.
[155]Moses Shtarkman, "Philip Krantz' Literary Encounters," in *Philological Writings,* Vol. 3, Vilna 1929, pp. 70-72.
[156]Ibid., p. 68.

larity to decide not to publish any further, and to keep one's promise for thirteen years!

* * * * *

Jacob Dinezon was far from being an overly agreeable sort if in 1907 he wrote, referring to the placid "Hershele's Songs": "The habit of Yiddish writers is—why should we deny it—much din and racket. . . . So that it appears to thunder; and the public, the simpletons, should immediately say a blessing: He is the Creator or His might and power fill the world."[157]

He had the courage to write *Samson Solomon and His Horses*, although writing such a story at that time in Tsarist Russia endangered one's life.[158]

And he—who so sought the friendship of all Yiddish writers—did not feel disturbed by writing about Reb Leybele the wine dealer, which is a fable and parable about those types of popular writers in which the writers are compared to dealers who have barely one type of poor wine, but for the public, it seems, they possess all sorts of wines from around the world. There is nothing that they don't have: Bordeaux, Madeira, Carmel wine. But the truth is the truth: "There is only faith, a strong faith in oneself, in the barrel, and in the other person's ignorance. Faith in oneself, faith in the inkwell, and faith in the ignorance of the reader who doesn't know the difference between Bordeaux, Sherry, or Madeira. How can one do this, I would ask myself, without deception? One cannot doubt for a moment that the one who drinks the wine, or the one who reads the literature, is an expert in these things: what is wine and what is literature."[159]

Jacob Dinezon trusted the reader. Therefore, the reader must prove his loyalty through appreciation and respect.

---

[157]"World of Books," Warsaw 1922, No. 3, *From Jacob Dinezon to Isaac Katzenelson.*
[158]"This remarkable period," it says in the introduction to the new edition of 1909, "roused all of Russia . . . and it flies off the shelf."
[159]"Deception," *Memories and Scenes*, pp. 209-210.

ACKNOWLEDGMENTS

We wish to thank Abraham Lichtenbaum and the Confederacion Pro Cultura Judia—Fundación IWO for permission to publish this English translation of *Yaakov Dinezon: Di mame tsvishn unzere klasikers*. Early support and help in tracking down the rights were provided by Samuel Rollansky's grandson, Eliezer Nowodworski, whose mother, Esther Rollansky, expressed an interest in having her father's work translated into English. Thanks also to Professor Alan Alto of Trinity University in San Antonio, Texas, for his help in tracking down Rollansky's heirs in Israel.

Our grateful appreciation to Miri Koral for her wonderful translation skills and professional interactions. Appreciation, also, to Arthur Clark and Lynn Padgett for their proofreading assistance and manuscript suggestions.

And finally, my sincerest gratitude to my sister Robin Evans for her partnership in bringing Jacob Dinezon's works into the 21st century, and to my sweet companion Carolyn Toben for her ongoing advice, encouragement, and unfailing optimism.

Scott Hilton Davis

GLOSSARY

Baba Bukh. A romance written in verse by Eliahu Bakhur in the 16th century; an important early poetic work in Old Yiddish.

belletrist. A writer of *belles lettres*; someone who creates literary works that are valued more for their aesthetic qualities than for their informational or educational content.

cheder. Traditional religious school for young boys.

chutzpah. Nerve, gall, or audacity.

Eastern Wall. The synagogue wall that faces east, which is the direction of Jerusalem for Jews living in the Diaspora; a place of honor in the synagogue.

Haskalah. The Jewish Enlightenment movement.

hasid. A follower of the Hasidic movement.

jargon. What Yiddish was called before it became a more acceptable Jewish language for literature and communications. Yiddish was also called "*di mame-loshn,*" the mother language or mother tongue.

kibitzer. A person who offers advise or criticism.

kosher. Food prepared according to Jewish law.

kreplach. Small dumplings filled with meat or another filling.

lamed-vovnik. One of the thirty-six hidden saints or holy ones whose piety and righteous merit sustains the world.

maskil. A follower of the Jewish Enlightenment movement.

minyan. Ten men needed to hold a public Jewish prayer service.

Musar. A non-Hasidic Jewish ethical, educational, and cultural movement founded in response to the Jewish Enlightenment movement.

rabiner. A rabbi.

rebbe. A teacher; also a Hasidic spiritual leader.

Shekhinah. The feminine, indwelling presence of the Divine on earth.

shmone esrey. Literally, "Eighteen"; the eighteen blessings recited three times a day in silence or in a whisper as part of the ritual prayers.

shmendrik. A silly or stupid person.

shokhet. A ritual slaughterer of animals and poultry.

Tsene Rene. A late 16th century Yiddish prayer book commonly called the "Women's Bible" that contains readings that correspond to the weekly Torah portions of the Pentateuch and Haftorah.

vastreger. A water carrier.

Yiddishist. A proponent of Yiddish language and culture.

zeitgeist. The spirit of the times; the ideas, beliefs, and mood of a particular historical period.

MEMORIES AND SCENES
SHTETL, CHILDHOOD WRITERS

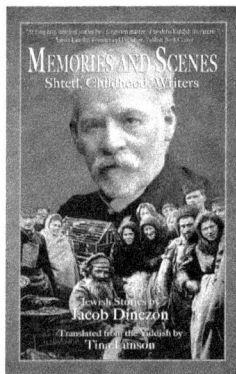

This collection of eleven autobiographical short stories by the beloved Yiddish writer Jacob Dinezon includes humorous and poignant experiences from his childhood in the shtetl, colorful characters that influenced his life, and the events that ignited his passion for writing.

A treasure trove of Jewish history, culture, and values available for the first time in English.

Translated from the Yiddish by Tina Lunson.

(ISBN 978-0-9798156-1-4)

HERSHELE
A JEWISH LOVE STORY

When Hershele, a poor but brilliant yeshiva student, is invited for a weekly charity meal by a rich widow, he comes face-to-face with Mirele, the widow's pretty, bright, and strong-willed daughter. As the two innocently come to know each other, they fall in love.

Are they *bashert*—soul mates destined to be together? Or will rigid class differences, shtetl politics, and a ruthless marriage broker tear them apart?

A poignant love story written by the "Father of the Jewish Realistic Romance."

Translated from the Yiddish by Jane Peppler. Edited and with an introduction by Scott Hilton Davis.

(ISBN 978-0-9798156-7-6)

www.ingramcontent.com/pod-product-compliance
Lightning Source LLC
Chambersburg PA
CBHW031853090426
42741CB00005B/472